DISASTER SURVIVAL HANDBOOK

DISASTER SURVIVAL HANDBOOK

ALTON L. THYGERSON

Brigham Young University Press

to those most important to me—my family

Library of Congress Cataloging in Publication Data

Thygerson, Alton L
  Disaster survival handbook

  Includes index.
  1. Disaster relief—Handbooks, Manuals, etc.
2. Survival and emergency rations—Handbooks, manuals,
etc. 3.—Survival (after floods, tornadoes, fires,
etc.)—Handbooks, manuals, etc. I. Title.
HV553.T48   361.5'02'02   79-4242
ISBN 0-8425-1629-8

Portions of the book are adapted from the following United States government publications:

Department of Agriculture, *Avalanche Handbook and Family Food Stockpile for Survival*
Department of the Air Force, *Survival: Training Edition*
Department of Commerce, *Lightning; Tornado; Hurricane; Floods, Flash Floods, and Warnings; Heat Wave; Winter Storms;* and *Earthquakes*
Defense Civil Preparedness Agency, *Disaster Operations: A Handbook for Local Governments*
Department of Defense, *Protection in the Nuclear Age*
Department of Health, Education, and Welfare and Department of Defense, *Family Guide Emergency Health Care*

CONTENTS

PREFACE

Disasters may come about through the forces of nature or through man's manipulations, but that they will come is certain.

But where do we turn when these perils occur? The answer is that we should be self-reliant. This is not to say that we have no need of others. On the contrary, most of life's best experiences are derived from the support and affection we share with others. Self-reliance means exercising our developed abilities to do for ourselves what is rightly our responsibility.

However, we cannot effectively deal with disasters unless we know something about them. Individuals and families must have a guide for action.

This book will help people prepare to survive disasters. Unlike other disaster books (which mainly focus upon disaster accounts, wilderness survival tactics, and/or food storage and recipe ideas), the *Disaster Survival Handbook* (1) discusses the nature of disasters, (2) describes what to do before, during, and after each, and (3) details the techniques of both short- and long-term survival.

A book of this kind has to reflect the author's experience. First, like most Americans, I have been exposed to many of the disasters discussed. In addition, I have spent many years teaching disaster preparedness in my safety education and emergency-care courses at Brigham Young University. And I enjoy close associations with the National Safety Council and the American National Red Cross.

I have also drawn on my experience as author of the college textbook, *Accidents and Disasters: Causes and Countermeasures.* Finally, when I was considered for the expert's role on the nationally televised "National Disaster Survival Test," I recognized the public need for readily available disaster-survival information. And that clarified the need for this book.

The *Disaster Survival Handbook* will help you prepare for those calamities that happen altogether too frequently.

I am grateful to John Drayton and Lane Johnson, who through their editorial skills helped produce a better book. I am indebted to my sister Sherry Littler, who typed the original draft, and to Rich Holdaway, who prepared the drawings.

Alton L. Thygerson
Provo, Utah

INTRODUCTION

Today we are dependent on others for nearly all our needs. We exchange money for shelter, clothing, food, water, electricity, and transportation. Modern technology is what holds together the delicate fabric of our society.

But where does this leave us when an emergency turns our world into a wilderness? In a major disaster, we may be helpless to provide even the most basic of our needs—shelter, water, and food.

Disaster is a fact of life. Each year thousands of disasters, large and small, natural and man-made, strike somewhere in the United States. These catastrophes range from airplane crashes involving just a few casualties to hurricanes, tornadoes, and earthquakes with massive destruction. Most people will remember one or more of the disasters listed in Table 0-1.

Strangely enough, most people survive emergency disaster situations. Good luck and sheer willpower often have a lot to do with survival. One man, stranded without food or water on a vast stretch of Arizona desert for 8 days traveled 150 miles in daytime temperatures as high as 120 degrees. Lack of water caused him to lose 25 percent of his weight through dehydration (10 percent loss is often fatal). He had crawled the last 8 miles completely naked, and doctors found his blood to be so thick that the lacerations he suffered did not bleed until he had drunk a large amount of water. He had done nothing right, had no survival training. But he wanted to survive and he did survive, through nothing but willpower.

You will hear other stories of equally harrowing experiences. But don't accept them as models for practical survival. They merely show what can be done with no experience, thought, or training. Add skill and wise preparation to this will to survive, and you will increase manyfold your chances of coming through a catastrophe with.a minimum of suffering.

Training in disaster survival needs to be modified from a "nice-to-know" to a "must-know" requirement. When disaster strikes,

1

you must be ready to act. Now is the time for survival preparation.

This handbook is intended to help you think and plan now. It offers numerous valuable facts about disasters. For example:

- What kinds of disasters are to be expected? Hurricanes frequently visit the Gulf and Atlantic coasts; earthquakes occur more often in the West; a tornado belt extends from Texas to Wisconsin. But disasters do not follow hard and fast rules. Towns far from rivers have been flooded. Tornadoes have been reported in all 50 states at one time or another. Lightning can strike almost anywhere.

- What will be their characteristics? Driving winds and rains are characteristic of hurricanes, but knowing that hurricanes have a calm spot or "eye" in their center may prevent you from making the mistake of leaving shelter when the storm has gone only halfway by.

- When can disasters be expected? Floods are more common in the spring; tornadoes may come in the spring and summer months, and hurricanes in the late summer and early fall. Blizzards, which cause many deaths, come in the winter months. Other disasters (fire, etc.) are liable to occur at any time under certain conditions.

- What course of action will be useful? This handbook emphasizes the entire chronology of disasters, from the "pre-disaster phases" (advance preparation and early recognition of the threat), to the "impact phase" (what to do when the disaster actually strikes), to the "post-disaster phase" (which includes recovery from the disaster).

Careful use of this handbook will help you (1) avoid disasters or at least keep damage and injury to a minimum, (2) rescue victims and provide first aid and emergency care, and (3) use your knowledge of survival skills to get yourself and others through the aftermath of a disaster.

TABLE 0-1. DISASTERS RESULTING IN 100 OR MORE DEATHS RANKED BY DEATH TOLL IN THE UNITED STATES, 1941–78

Type of Accident	Place	Date	Number of Deaths
Fire and explosion	Texas City, Texas	April 16–17, 1947	561
Nightclub fire	Boston, Mass.	November 28, 1942	492
Hurricane and floods	Louisiana, Texas, and several other states	June 27–28, 1957	395
Explosion of two ammunition ships	Port Chicago, Calif.	July 18, 1944	322
Series of tornadoes	Midwest and South	April 3–4, 1974	307
Tornadoes	Midwest	April 11, 1965	272
Hurricane and subsequent floods	Mississippi, Louisiana, Virginia	August 17–20, 1969	256
Flash flood	Rapid City, S.D.	June 9, 1972	237
Series of tornadoes	Mississippi Valley states	March 21–22, 1952	229
Hurricane and floods	Northeastern United States	August 17–19, 1955	180
Circus fire	Hartford, Conn.	July 6, 1944	168
Fire in nightclub	Southgate, Ky.	May 28, 1977	164
Tornado	Texas and Oklahoma	April 9, 1947	167
Tornado	Pennsylvania, West Virginia, Maryland	June 23, 1944	159
Mid-air collision of two planes	Over San Diego, Calif.	Sept. 28, 1978	144
Series of tornadoes	Michigan and Ohio	June 8, 1953	142
Flash Flood	Big Thompson River Canyon, Colorado	July 31, 1976	145
Midair collision of two scheduled planes	Staten Island, New York	December 16, 1960	134
Gas tank explosion	Cleveland, Ohio	October 20, 1944	130
Midair collision of two scheduled planes	Over Grand Canyon, Ariz.	June 30, 1956	128
Collapse of dam made from mine wastes, flooding valley	Buffalo Creek, W. Va.	February 26, 1972	125
Tornadoes	Mississippi and Louisiana	February 21, 1971	121
Tornado	Oklahoma, Missouri, Arkansas	April 12, 1945	119
Hotel fire	Atlanta, Ga.	December 7, 1946	119
Coal mine explosion	West Frankfort, Ill.	December 21, 1951	119
Hurricane and subsequent floods	Eastern seaboard	June 19–28, 1972	118
Series of tornadoes	Kansas, Oklahoma, Texas, Missouri	May 25, 1955	115
Tornado	Waco, Texas	May 11, 1953	114
Earthquake	Alaska	March 27, 1964	114
Crash of scheduled plane	New York, N. Y.	June 24, 1975	113

3

Type of Accident	Place	Date	Number of Deaths
Tornadoes	Southern and midwestern states	March 17, 1942	111
Coal mine explosion	Centralia, Ill.	March 25, 1947	111
Crash of scheduled plane	Near Juneau, Alaska	September 4, 1971	111
Crash of scheduled plane	Near Miami, Fla.	December 29, 1972	101
Destroyer explosion	New York Bay, N. Y.	January 3, 1944	100
Wind and snowstorm	Northeastern United States	November 25, 1950	100
Hurricane	Atlantic coast and New England states	October 15, 1954	100

Note: Figures for natural disasters are approximate.
Adapted from the Metropolitan Insurance Company, *Statistical Bulletin*. By permission.

SECTION 1: DISASTERS

1. RIVER FLOODS

In popular usage, "river flood" simply describes an overflow of water from a river onto normally dry land. (Flooding resulting from hurricanes, tsunamis, and flash flooding is treated in other chapters.) More professionally, a river is "in flood" when its waters have risen to a height at which damage from the force of currents and inundation can occur in the absence of protective works.[1]

Devastating floods occur in almost every part of the United States, where an estimated 50 million acres are subject to flooding. Although this is only 2.5 percent of the total land area, most of it is densely populated and is of high value. Approximately 10 million people live in the significantly defined flood plains, and another 25 million nearby can be indirectly affected. For the United States in recent years, the average yearly death toll as a result of floods has been 83,[2] with annual losses in property damage totalling $1 billion.[3]

Certain areas such as the Pacific Northwest, the Rocky Mountain and Great Basin areas, and part of Southern California experience floods only during well-defined seasons. On the other hand, along the southeastern and Gulf coasts, floods occur without any pronounced seasonal pattern. There are yet other areas—the Northeast and in the basins of the Ohio and Mississippi rivers—where a great flood may occur at any time of the year but where most floods occur during a fairly well defined flooding season.

By analyzing records of stream flow and other data, the probable frequency of floods for a given river can be estimated. For example, a flood might be referred to as a "ten-year flood," meaning that a flood of this size occurs about once in ten years. However, it is impossible to predict accurately that such a flood will occur in any particular year. Major flood conditions occur about every two to four years in the larger river basins of the Ohio, Missouri, upper Mississippi, and Columbia rivers. By contrast, the 1965 flood of the South Platte River near Denver, Colorado, was the first in more than thirty years.

Flood Devastation

The immediate effects of floods are brought about by inundation and the force of currents. People and livestock may be injured or drowned. Roadbeds are vulnerable to scouring action (sidewash) and undermining if they lie parallel to the flow, and to overflow if they lie across the flow. Even roadbeds well above the crest of a flood may be undermined by scouring and collapsed by slides. Bridge abutments are vulnerable to currents and current-borne debris. Airport runways, highways, and city streets can suffer damage from immersion and be made useless for a time by high water and deposits of mud and debris. Sanitary, power, water, gas, and telephone installations are damaged and systems interrupted. Business inventories and personal belongings are lost or damaged. Farms can lose stored feed, equipment, and buildings. The farmlands may be deeply eroded by new channels or denuded of valuable topsoil, crops, and other vegetation. Even those buildings that can withstand serious structural damage can suffer damage to exterior and interior surfaces, furnishings, and contents.

Flood damage can lead to hunger, disease, and costly deprivations. Many people are left homeless. Forced evacuations can separate family members. Transportation, communication, and rescue services can be seriously disrupted—when medical emergencies are at a peak. Water may be contaminated through broken water and sanitary systems. Wild animals and snakes may be driven into inhabited areas, and rats forced from their regular habitats can cause particular health problems.

Floods in the Making

Although floods are notoriously unpredictable—some providing ample warning, others taking the countryside by surprise—conditions that give rise to flooding are generally well known.

Floods occur when water rises and forms a temporary channel over lands normally used for human habitation. The primary sources of this excess water are abnormally heavy rainfall and runoff from large accumulations of packed snow. Flooding from snowpack is caused by rising temperatures, sometimes accompanied by rainfall, that melt the snow rapidly.

A drastic increase in water runoff from watersheds is frequently the result of conditions brought about by both man and nature.

8

Flood waters. *Courtesy American National Red Cross.*

Forest or brush fires destroy the ground cover so essential to drainage slopes. Man also denudes the watershed by cutting trees, by clearing the land, or by overgrazing. Careless agricultural practices also contribute to the problem.

3. Serious flooding in the lower reaches of large rivers occurs when flood crests from major tributaries arrive simultaneously. For example, floods in the lower Mississippi River frequently follow the arrival of flood crests from two or more major tributaries—the Ohio River, the Tennessee-Cumberland complex, the Missouri River, and the upper Mississippi.

Flooding can also occur when ice jams block the river flow. The jams are caused by weather and currents that break up the river ice but fail to clear the channel. Initially, stoppages cause flooding upstream; later, when the ice jam breaks, the flooding occurs downstream.

4. History is replete with disasters resulting from dam failures. Poor construction can have disastrous results, as certainly was the case in the 1963 failure of the Baldwin Hills Reservoir in Los Angeles County, California, which caused property damage in the millions of dollars. Another example is the 1976 collapse of the Teton Dam in Idaho, which killed eleven and caused many millions of dollars of property damage.

Landslides, avalanches, and earthquakes also can trigger disastrous floods. Landslides have blocked channels and inundated upstream areas. Hebgen Lake, Montana, was created by a slide that occurred during a 1959 earthquake. The possibility of future dam failure is of particular concern, because the best dam sites are often in valleys created by early geologic upheavals—where such activity could well recur. In California, for example, some dam structures have actually been built across parts of the San Andreas fault system, with one side anchored to the Pacific geologic plate and the other resting on the continental plate of North America. The hazards of living below such a dam hardly need elaboration.

Suggested Procedures

A sensible way to prepare for possible floods begins with being aware of general conditions where you live. Suppose, for example, that you live by a river that is fed by a mountain watershed, and suppose that the watershed was stripped of vegetation by a forest fire last summer and then covered by a heavy snowpack during the winter. These are facts you should be aware of. Suppose further that in the springtime the temperature soars and a warm rain moves into the mountains. Under these extreme conditions you should definitely be on the alert.

Through its river forecast centers and river district offices, the National Weather Service issues flood forecasts and warnings when rainfall is heavy enough to cause rivers to overflow their banks and when melting snow may combine with rainfall to produce flooding.

Flood warnings are forecasts of impending floods, and are distributed to the public by radio and through local government emergency forces. The warning message tells the expected severity of flooding (minor, moderate, or major), the affected river, and when and where flooding will begin. Careful preparations and prompt response will reduce property loss and ensure personal safety.

Flash flood warnings are the most urgent type of flood warning issued, and are also transmitted to the public over radio, television, and by other signals (e.g., sirens) established by local government to meet local needs.

To help you further prepare for the possibility of floods in your area, the following procedures are suggested:

Before a Flood

- Find out how many feet your property is above or below possible flood levels, so that when predicted flood levels are broadcast you can determine whether or not you may be flooded. Also locate the nearest safe area.
- Keep a stock of food that requires little cooking and no refrigeration; electric and gas power may be interrupted. Keeping a small emergency supply of food that can be moved quickly to your automobile is also a good precaution.
- Keep a portable radio, emergency cooking equipment, and flashlights in working order.
- Keep first aid and critical medical supplies (prescription drugs, insulin, etc.) at hand.
- Keep your automobile fueled. If electric power is cut off, service stations may not be able to operate pumps for several days.
- Keep sandbags, plywood, plastic sheeting, and lumber handy for emergency waterproofing.

When You Receive a Flood Warning

- Store drinking water in closed, clean containers. Water service may be interrupted.
- Move food, water, and other emergency supplies to your automobile.
- If flooding is likely, and time permits, move essential items and furniture to upper floods of your house.
- Turn off all electric circuits at the fuse panel or disconnect all electrical appliances. Shut off the water service and gas valves in your home.
- *Above all,* move to a safe area *before* access is cut off by floodwaters.

During a Flood

- Stay on higher ground; avoid areas subject to sudden flooding.
- Do not attempt to cross a flowing stream when the water is above your knees.
- Do not attempt to drive over a flooded road. You can be stranded and trapped.
- If your vehicle stalls, abandon it immediately and seek higher ground. Many people drown while trying to rescue their car.

After a Flood

- Do not use fresh food that has come in contact with flood waters.
- Test drinking water for potability. Wells should be pumped out and the water tested before drinking.
- Do not visit disaster areas; your presence will probably hamper rescue and other emergency operations.
- Do not handle live electrical equipment in wet areas. Electrical equipment should be checked and dried thoroughly before being returned to service.
- To examine buildings, use flashlights, *not* lanterns or torches: flammables from broken containers or ruptured gas lines may be inside.
- Report broken utility lines to the power company or to a police or fire department.
- Keep tuned to radio or television stations for (1) instructions on where to obtain medical care and emergency assistance such as housing, clothing, and food, and (2) ways to help yourself and your community recover from the emergency.

Notes

1. Gilbert F. White, *Human Adjustment to Floods* (Chicago: University of Chicago Press, 1945), p. 37.
2. U.S. Department of Commerce, National Oceanic and Atmospheric Administration (NOAA), Environmental Data Service, *Climatological Data, National Summary, 1970* (Asheville, N.C., 1971), p. 94.
3. U.S. Department of Commerce, Office of Hydrology, *A Plan for Improving the National River and Flood Forecast and Warning Service* (Silver Spring, Md., December 1969), p. 13.

2. FLASH FLOODS

On June 9, 1972, thunderstorms settled over the Black Hills of South Dakota, resulting in flash floods that took the lives of more than 200 people in and near Rapid City.

In 1976 a tremendous flash flood roared through Big Thompson River Canyon, Colorado. The effects of heavy thunderstorms (which remained stationary for many hours because of an unusual absence of wind) were magnified by the narrowness of the canyon and the steepness of its sides, causing the water level to rise rapidly and making escape difficult for the thousands of campers, fishermen, motorists, and other vacationers in the area. One hundred forty-five died.

As in river floods, inundation and currents are the primary destructive forces. In flash floods, however, the swift currents can be especially vicious; and the potential for frightful devastation is compounded by the fact that flash floods often occur with little or no warning. Overtaken suddenly by a wall of churning water and debris, people and animals are swept downstream, injured, and drowned. In recent years, flash floods have taken an average of more than 100 lives a year and have been reported in almost every region of the United States. (Figure 2-1.)

In urban areas, where the flood plain has been converted to buildings, roads, and parking lots, heavy rains produce flash flooding severe enough to wash away cars and inflict heavy damage to residential and industrial buildings at lower ground levels.

Most flash floods occur in mountainous areas, where torrential thunderstorms can change trickling brooks into raging torrents. Most susceptible are the upper reaches of streams and creeks in regions where thunderstorms frequently occur in spring and summer.

On small streams, especially near the headwaters of river basins, water levels may rise quickly in heavy rainstorms, and flash floods can begin before the rain stops falling.

In 1970, 11 inches of rain within 24 hours produced a terrifying flash flood in Arizona. The rates at which streams rose were de-

Flash-flood rescue operations. *Courtesy National Oceanic and Atmospheric Administration.*

Figure 2-1. Sites of significant flash floods. *National Oceanic and Atmospheric Administration.*

scribed as unbelievable. Uprooted trees, huge boulders, fences, automobiles, and small buildings were swept downstream. Twenty-three lives were lost.

Rainfall of more than four inches in a few hours is recorded many times each year; in the United States the record rainfall for one hour exceeds 10 inches. Under such conditions there is little time between detection of flood conditions and the arrival of the flood crest. Swift action is essential.

Suggested Procedures

Before a flood, know the elevation of your property in relation to nearby streams and other waterways, and make advance plans for what you will do and where you will go in a flash flood emergency.

When a Flash Flood Watch Is Issued for Your Area

- Listen to area radio and television stations for flash flood warnings and reports of flooding in progress.
- Be prepared to move out of danger's way at a moment's notice.
- Leave *without delay* if you are warned that a flash flood is coming your way.

During a Flash Flood

- Stay away from flooded areas.
- If you are in your vehicle don't try to drive it through water of unknown depth. If your vehicle stalls, abandon it immediately and seek higher ground; rapidly rising water may sweep away the vehicle and its occupants. Many deaths have been caused by attempts to move stalled vehicles.
- At night, when it is harder to recognize flood dangers, be especially cautious.
- When you are out of immediate danger, tune in area radio or television stations for additional information as conditions change and new reports are received.

After the Flash Flood Watch or Warning Is Cancelled

Stay tuned to radio or television for follow-up information. Flash flooding may have ended, but general flooding may come later in headwater streams and major rivers. Remember: any heavy rain can cause locally destructive flash flooding. When it is raining, think flash floods.

When You Go into Remote Areas

- Inform someone of your destination and when you expect to return. Police should be notified immediately if you do not return on time.
- Take survival supplies for several days, including food, water, first-aid equipment, and necessary medications.
- Stay away from natural streambeds, arroyos, and other drainage channels during and after rainstorms. Water runs off the higher elevations very rapidly.
- Use your maps. Know where you are and whether you are on locally low ground. Know where the high ground is and how to get there.
- Remember: you don't have to be at the bottom of a hill to be a target for flash flood dangers. Following heavy rains in Southern California in early 1971, a gigantic flash flood roaring down a canyon into Death Valley left huge sections of the paved highway stranded well over a hundred feet up the hillside.
- Stay out of flooded areas.
- Keep alert for signs of wet weather, either rain where you are or signs of rain—thunder and lightning—nearby. A thunderstorm cloud, called cumulonimbus, is a large towering cloud, frequently spreading out on top in the shape of an anvil. It usually appears dark and threatening when viewed from below, but very bright and white when seen from the side at some distance.
- Follow the instructions of local authorities. If you are warned to leave an area—*leave.* Many lives have been lost needlessly because people refused to heed the warnings of police officers, park rangers, and other officials.

3. TORNADOES

The tornado is a violent local storm with whirling winds of tremendous speed. It appears as a rotating, whirlpool-shaped cloud that extends toward the ground from the base of a thundercloud—the familiar and frightening tornado funnel. From gray to black in color, the tornado spins like a top and may sound like the roaring of an airplane or a locomotive. It is from the twisting spiral updraft that tornadoes have been dubbed "twisters." These small, short-lived storms are the most violent of all storms and, over a small area, the most destructive.

The dark funnel can destroy solid buildings, make a deadly missile of a piece of straw, uproot large trees, and hurl people and animals for hundreds of yards.

Tornadoes do their destructive work through the combined action of strong rotary winds, flying debris, and the partial vacuum in the center of the vortex. As a tornado passes over a building, the winds twist and rip at the outside walls, while the reduced pressure in the tornado's "eye" causes an explosive pressure difference between the inside and outside of the building. Walls collapse or topple outward, windows explode, and the resulting debris is driven through the air in a dangerous barrage. Overhead power and telephone lines are cut and poles snapped. Mature trees are often snapped in two or uprooted. Crops, livestock, and farm dwellings bear the brunt of the tornadoes in rural areas. Heavy objects, such as machinery and railroad cars, are lifted and carried by the wind for considerable distances. In 1931, for example, a tornado in Minnesota carried a railroad coach (weighing 183 tons, with 117 passengers aboard) some 80 feet through the air before dropping it into a ditch.[1]

People are highly vulnerable. Often with little or no warning and in a matter of seconds, a tornado can transform a thriving street into a ruin. Death and injury result from the disintegration or collapse of buildings, debris driven by the high winds, flash flooding caused by the accompanying downpour, and electrocution on fallen utility lines.

Although the life of a tornado is short and its destruction path relatively small, this type of storm has destroyed much property and taken many lives, especially in densely populated areas. For example, on April 3, 1974, more than 100 tornadoes ripped through eleven states in the South and Midwest, causing 318 deaths in the United States and 8 in Canada.[2]

Tornadoes are most likely to be killers when they are least expected. *Courtesy National Oceanic and Atmospheric Administration.*

A Nationwide Threat

Tornadoes are almost exclusively an American problem; they have been reported in areas outside the United States, but not often. In the United States they have occurred in all fifty states, in every season of the year.

Normally, the number of tornadoes is lowest during December and January and highest in May. In February, when tornado activity begins to increase, maximum frequency occurs over the central Gulf states. During March, the area of maximum frequency moves eastward to the southeast Atlantic states, where tornado occurrence reaches a peak in April. During May the center of activity moves to the southern Plains states and, in June, northward to the northern Plains and Great Lakes areas and even as far eastward as western New York state. The reason for these shifts is the increasing penetration of warm, moist air from the south into the continental land mass at the same time as contrasting cool, dry air is surging in from the north and northwest. Tornadoes occur most often where these air masses meet and collide.

Although records of tornadoes in the United States have been kept for a long time, a reliable statistical history of these disturbances dates back only to 1953, when the U.S. Department of Commerce began its tornado forecasting. For example, from 1916 through 1952, fewer than 300 tornadoes were reported in any one year. In 1953, however, more than 437 tornadoes were observed and reported; since then, the number has never fallen below that level for any one year. From 1953 through 1970, an average of 622 tornadoes occurred each year in the United States, about half of them during April, May, and June. Average annual frequency by states for this period ranges from 104 tornadoes in Texas to fewer than three in most of the northeastern and far western states. (See Figure 3-1.)

Loss of life and property from windstorms has also been considerable. For example, in the United States the death figure attributable to this phenomenon closely approximates total deaths from tornadoes. It is interesting to note that approximately 20 percent of all deaths resulting from windstorms occurred in one year, 1928.

Tornadoes may occur at any hour of the day or night, but they form most readily during the warmest hours of the day. Most tornadoes (82 percent) occur between noon and midnight, and the

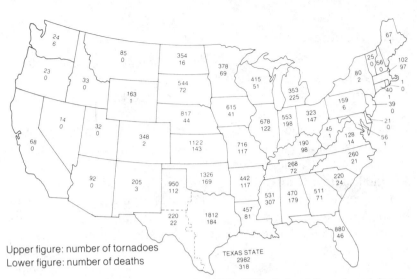

Figure 3-1. Tornado Incidence and deaths, 1953–1976. *National Oceanic and Atmospheric Administration.*

Upper figure: number of tornadoes
Lower figure: number of deaths

greatest single concentration (23 percent) falls between 4:00 and 6:00 P.M.

The probability that a specific location will be struck by a tornado in any one year is quite small. For example, the chance of a tornado's striking a given point in the area most frequently subject to tornadoes is about once in 350 years. In the far western states, the probability is close to zero. But there are exceptions. Oklahoma City has been struck by tornadoes 26 times since 1892. Baldwyn, Mississippi, was struck twice by tornadoes during a 25 minute period on March 16, 1942. A third of Irving, Kansas, was left in ruins by two tornadoes which occurred 45 minutes apart on May 30, 1879. Austin, Texas, had two tornadoes in rapid succession on May 4, 1922; and Codell, Kansas, was struck on the same date—May 20—in three consecutive years: 1916, 1917, and 1918.[3]

The Formation of a Tornado

Tornadoes typically form during warm, humid, unsettled weather when there is a squall line of severe thunderstorms.

Currently scientists seem to agree that tornadoes are created when cool air overrides a layer of warm air. As the warm air rises rapidly through the cool air, a rotary flow forms and produces a spiral air flow. Then, if the vortex persists, external forces reduce the radius of rotation and, in so doing, increase the speed of rotation—in the same way that an ice skater increases his speed of rotation by drawing in his arms. Ultimately, the rising, converging, rotating winds accelerate to form the tornado.

Sometimes two or more tornadoes are associated with a parent thunderstorm. As the thunderstorm moves, tornadoes may form at intervals along its path, travel for a few miles, and then dissipate.

The forward speed of tornadoes has been observed to range from almost no motion to 70 miles per hour. On the average, tornado paths are only an eighth of a mile wide and are seldom more than 10 miles long. However, there have been spectacular instances in which tornadoes have caused heavy destruction along paths more than a mile wide and almost 300 miles long. A tornado traveled 293 miles across the states of Illinois and Indiana on May 26, 1917, lasting 7 hours and 20 minutes. Its forward speed was 40 miles per hour, an average figure for tornadoes.[4] One of the more than 50 tornadoes that ripped through the Mississippi delta on February 21, 1971, traveled 159 miles. Its speed was 55 miles per hour.[5]

If the atmospheric conditions occur over a large body of water, the vortex phenomenon is referred to as a "waterspout." Instead of the dust and debris found over land, the funnel cloud usually consists of water spray.

Suggested Procedures

Knowing what to do when a tornado is approaching may mean the difference between life and death. If you see any revolving, funnel-shaped clouds on a cloudy day, report them by telephone immediately to the local police department, sheriff's office, or National Weather Service office. But do not use the telephone to get information and advice—depend on your radio or television. The National Weather Service issues severe weather warnings to the public, and these are broadcast over radio and TV.

A *tornado watch* means tornadoes are expected to develop.

A *tornado warning* means a tornado has actually been sighted or indicated on radar.

When a Tornado Watch Is Announced

- Keep your radio or television on and listen for the latest National Weather Service warnings and advisories. If power fails, use a battery-operated radio or your car radio.

21

- Keep watching the sky, especially to the south and southwest. (However, when a tornado watch is announced during the approach of a *hurricane,* keep in mind that a tornado may move from an easterly directly.)

When a Tornado Warning Is Announced

- Your best protection is an underground shelter or cave, or a steel-framed or reinforced concrete building. If none is available, take refuge in other places as indicated below.
- If your home has no basement, take cover under heavy furniture on the ground floor in the center of the house, or in a small ground-floor room away from outside walls and windows. As a last resort, go outside to a nearby ditch, excavation, culvert, or ravine.
- Doors and windows on the sides of your house away from the tornado may be left open to help reduce damage to the building, but stay away from them to avoid flying debris.
- Do not remain in a trailer or mobile home if a tornado is approaching. Take cover elsewhere.
- If advised that you are likely to be in the path of a tornado, and if time permits, turn off electricity and fuel lines.
- If you are outside in open country, drive away from the tornado's path, at a right angle to it. If there isn't time to do this— or if you are walking—take cover and lie flat in the nearest depression, such as a ditch, culvert, excavation, or ravine.
- Schools. If the school building is of good steel-reinforced construction, stay inside away from the windows and remain near an inside wall on the lower floors if possible. *Avoid auditoriums and gymnasiums* with large, poorly supported roofs. In rural schools that do not have reinforced construction, move schoolchildren and teachers to a ravine or ditch if storm shelters are not available.
- Factories and Industrial Plants. When possible, shut off electrical circuits and fuel lines if a tornado approaches the plant. Workers should be moved to sections offering the best possible protection, in accordance with advance plans.
- Shopping Centers. Go to a designated shelter area, *not* to your parked car.
- Office Buildings. Go to an interior hallway on the lowest floor, or to a designated shelter area. Stay away from windows.

Tornado destruction of mobile homes. *Courtesy National Oceanic and Atmospheric Administration.*

After a Tornado Passes

- Use extreme caution in entering or working in buildings that may have been damaged or weakened by the disaster; they may collapse without warning. Also, live electrical circuits may be exposed.
- Don't take lanterns, torches, or lighted cigarettes into buildings damaged by a natural disaster. There may be leaking gas lines or flammable material.

- Stay away from fallen or damaged electrical wires. They may still be dangerous.
- Check for leaking gas pipes in your home. Do this by smell—*not with matches or candles.* If you smell gas: (1) open all windows and doors; (2) leave the house immediately; (3) turn off the main gas valve at the meter; (4) notify the gas company or the police or fire department; and (5) remain outside the house until you are told it is safe to reenter.
- If any of your electrical appliances are wet, first turn off the main power switch in your house, then unplug the wet appliance, dry it out, reconnect it, and finally, turn on the main power switch. (Caution: Don't do any of these things while you are wet or standing in water.) If fuses blow when the electric power is restored, turn off the main power switch immediately and inspect for short circuits in your home wiring, appliances, and equipment.
- Check your food and water supplies before using them. Foods that require refrigeration may be spoiled if electric power has been off for some time.
- Stay away from disaster areas. Sightseeing could interfere with first-aid or rescue work—and may be dangerous as well.
- Don't drive unless necessary, and if you must, drive with caution. Watch for hazards to yourself and others, and report them to local police or fire departments.
- Report broken sewer or water mains to the water utility department.
- Keep tuned to your radio or television stations for instructions on where to obtain necessary medical care, where to obtain emergency assistance for housing, clothing, and food, and how to help yourself and your community recover from the emergency.

Constructing a Storm Cellar

Where tornadoes are frequent, a shelter is vital. The shelter may never be needed, but during a tornado emergency it will be worth the effort of preparing it. One of the safest tornado shelters is an underground excavation known as a storm cellar. The following are suggestions for building a storm cellar.
- Location. When possible, the storm cellar should be outside and near the residence, but not so close that falling walls or

debris could block the exit. If there is a rise in the ground, the cellar may be dug into it to make use of the rise for protection. The cellar should not be connected in any way with house drains, cesspools, or sewer and gas pipes.

- Size. The size of the shelter depends on the number of persons to be accommodated and the storage needs. A structure 8 feet long by 6 feet wide and 7 feet high will protect eight people for a short time and provide limited storage space.
- Material. Reinforced concrete is the best material for a tornado shelter. Other suitable building materials include split logs, 2-inch planks (treated with creosote and covered with tar paper), cinder block, hollow tile, and brick. The roof should be covered with a 3-foot mound of well-pounded dirt, sloped to divert surface water. The entrance door should be of heavy construction.
- Drainage. The floor should slope to a drainage outlet if the terrain permits. If not, a dry well can be dug. An outside drain is better, because it will aid ventilation.
- Ventilation. A vertical ventilating shaft about 1 foot square can extend from near the floor level through the ceiling. This can be converted into an emergency escape hatch if the opening through the ceiling is made 2 feet square and the 1-foot shaft below is made easily removable. Slat gratings of heavy wood on the floor also will improve air circulation.
- Emergency Equipment. A lantern and tools—crowbar, pick, shovel, hammer, pliers, screwdriver—should be stored in the cellar to ensure escape if cellar exits are blocked by debris. Stored metal tools should be greased to prevent rusting.

Notes

1. U.S. Department of Commerce, National Oceanic and Atmospheric Administration (NOAA), *Tornado* (Washington, D.C.: U.S. Government Printing Office, 1970).
2. Metropolitan Life Insurance Company, *Statistical Bulletin,* January 1975, p. 6.
3. *Tornado.*
4. *Tornado.*
5. U.S. Department of Commerce, National Oceanic and Atmospheric Administration (NOAA), *Mississippi Delta Tornadoes of February 21, 1971,* Natural Disaster Survey Report 71-2 (Washington, D.C.: U.S. Government Printing Office, July 1971), pp. iii, 5.

Hurricane—wind and waves. *Courtesy National Oceanic and Atmospheric Administration.*

4. HURRICANES

A hurricane is a large spiral of winds blowing at speeds of 74 miles per hour or higher around a relatively calm center—the "eye." Hurricanes can be compared to giant whirlwinds in which air moves in a large, tightening spiral about a center of extreme low pressure.

Formed over warm ocean areas, these storms bear names given locally: *baguio* in the Philippines, *cyclone* in the Indian Ocean, *typhoon* in the Pacific. In our hemisphere, the name for this type of storm is *hurricane.* Some people erroneously refer to tornadoes as cyclones, but that term should not be applied to a tornado, twister, or waterspout.

The practice of naming hurricanes with girls' names began during World War II and was the official National Weather Service policy from 1953 to 1978. Now, however, the practice is to use male and female names alternately. The first tropical storm of a season is given a name beginning with the letter *A,* then the second storm's name begins with a *B,* and so on.

As in other weather-related disasters, the vulnerability of people and property to hurricanes is far reaching.

Usually people are most vulnerable to the ravages of hurricanes during the initial phase. Death and injury usually result from drowning, flying debris, and electrocution on downed utility lines.

Property damage is caused by high winds, rain, and flooding. Winds uproot trees and damage the roofs of buildings. As a result, rain enters the buildings, further damaging the interiors. Floods destroy crops, livestock, personal possessions, and real property. After the waters recede, they leave behind mud silt that compounds the damage and the rehabilitation costs.

Boarding up residences and business establishments in anticipation of the hurricane is costly—as is the dismantling. And the closure of many business and community activities incurs further loss of income.

The Anatomy of a Hurricane

The hurricane is unique in both structure and strength. On the average, the area that contains winds with speeds of at least 74 miles per hour covers some 100 miles in diameter, while gale-force winds—exceeding 40 miles per hour—extend over an area 400 miles in diameter.[1] Its spiral—counterclockwise in the Northern Hemisphere and clockwise in the Southern Hemisphere—is marked by heavy cloud bands, some containing very heavy rains and some only light rains or none at all. Lightning is visible in these bands.

Hurricane winds, like all winds, are produced by differences in atmospheric pressure. However, the pressure produced in hurricanes is the most severe in the atmosphere—excepting only the pressure change across the narrow funnel of a tornado.

The eye is unique to the hurricane; no other atmospheric phenomenon has this virtually calm core. The average eye diameter is about 14 miles, but diameters of 25 miles are not unusual. Here, winds are light and skies are clear or partly cloudy. But this calm is deceptive, bordered as it is by hurricane-force winds and torrential rains. (Many persons have been killed or injured when the calm eye lured them out of shelter only to be caught in the hurricane winds at the far side of the eye.) Near the eye, hurricane winds may gust to more than 200 miles per hour.

Over the years, the toll in lives exacted by hurricanes has diminished encouragingly. In the United States this reduction has resulted primarily from timely warnings. Damage to fixed property, however, continues to mount as areas affected by hurricanes undergo further extensive economic development. Most death and destruction is caused by wind, floods, and—most lethal of all—storm surges.

Wind

As winds increase in velocity, horizontal pressure against structures mounts with the square of wind velocity, so that a tenfold increase in wind speed increases the wind-created force a hundredfold. For example, a 25-mile-per-hour wind causes pressure of about 2 pounds per square foot on a flat surface; a wind of 200 miles per hour causes pressure of about 130 pounds per square foot. For most structures, such an added force is sufficient to cause failure. Hurricanes may also lower the atmospheric pressure outside a closed structure enough to cause normal pressure inside to explode outward and collapse the building. Tall structures like radio towers, buffeted by gusting hurricane-force winds, may oscillate until structural failure occurs.

Floods

Floods produced by hurricane rainfall are usually more destructive than the winds. The typical hurricane brings 6 to 12 inches of rainfall to the area it crosses, often in a few hours. The resulting floods produce great damage and loss of life, particularly in mountainous areas.

The winds from Hurricane Diane (1955), for example, caused little damage as they moved onto the continent. Long after the winds had subsided, however, floods produced by rainfall in Pennsylvania, New York, and New England killed 200 people and caused an estimated $700 million in damage.

Another example was Hurricane Camille in August 1969. Two days after this severe storm had wrecked the Louisiana-Mississippi coastline, its remnants dumped record-breaking amounts of rainfall in the mountains of western Virginia. The resultant flash floods claimed over 200 lives and caused more than $100 million in damages.

Storm Surges

The hurricane's worst killer is storm surges—wind-driven waters that sweep over low-lying coastal areas. More than 6,000 persons perished from a storm surge that devastated Galveston, Texas, in 1900; some 2,000 persons drowned in Florida in 1928 when the waters of Lake Okeechobee were literally blown out of their shallow basin; and about 380 drowned when Hurricane Audrey struck Louisiana in June 1957.

Over the deep ocean, the reduced atmospheric pressure in the storm center may actually draw the ocean surface upward (like water in a giant straw) a foot or so above normal. This creates large swells—reaching heights of 50 feet—on the ocean's surface. Thus, a hurricane's presence may be detected well in advance of its arrival on land by sea swells emanating from the storm.

As the storm crosses the continental shelf and moves toward the coast, mean water level may rise 15 feet or more. Behind the storm center, offshore hurricane-force winds may cause a decrease in mean water level, setting up strong currents. The advancing storm surge may be superimposed on normal astronomical tides, and, in turn, wind waves are superimposed on the surge. This buildup of water level can produce severe flooding in coastal areas, particularly when the storm surge coincides with normal high tides.

Much of the densely populated Atlantic and Gulf coasts lies within 10 feet of sea level and is therefore vulnerable to storm surges. Extended pounding by giant waves of water weighing some 1,700 pounds per cubic yard can demolish any structure not designed to withstand such forces. Currents, set up along the coast by storm-surge water heights, and the combined wind and wave actions erode foundations and topple buildings. And these same forces severely erode beaches and highways. A surge forced up a narrow channel, such as a riverbed, may appear as a wall of water—incorrectly called a "tidal wave"—engulfing everything in its passage.

A Seasonal Threat

Most hurricanes form in a belt between 8 and 15 degrees north and south of the Equator. Within this zone, the most likely areas of formation are those in which the surface water temperature is high, such as the Caribbean Sea.

The North Atlantic, the Caribbean Sea, and the Gulf of Mexico produce the hurricanes that ultimately affect the Gulf and East coasts of the United States. Most hurricanes occur in the North Atlantic and adjacent waters during August, September, and October.

Along the Atlantic and Gulf coasts, the normal hurricane season extends from June through November. Early in the season the Caribbean and the Gulf of Mexico are the principle areas of origin. In July and August this center shifts eastward, and by September it spreads from the Bahamas southeastward to the Lesser Antilles and eastward to the Cape Verde Islands off the west coast of Africa. After mid-September the major points of origin shift back to the western Caribbean and the Gulf of Mexico.

The record number of Atlantic hurricanes in a single season is 21. If the hurricane is an August storm, its average life expectancy is 12 days; if a July or November storm, it lives an average of 8 days.

Suggested Procedures

Because the amount of energy associated with hurricanes is so immense, there is as yet no satisfactory way of modifying or controlling them. Our best hope is that with early warning and other precautionary measures we can minimize losses in human life and property. When hurricanes are approaching the United States mainland, the National Weather Service issues early warnings.

A *hurricane watch* means that a hurricane *may* threaten an area within 24 hours. A hurricane watch is *not* a hurricane warning, but a first alert for emergency forces and the general public in areas that may be threatened. When your area is under a hurricane watch, you should continue normal activities but stay tuned to radio or television stations for all Weather Service advisories.

A *hurricane warning* means that a hurricane is expected to strike an area within 24 hours. Advisories containing hurricane warnings include an assessment of flood danger in coastal and inland areas, small-craft warnings, gale warnings for the storm's periphery, estimated storm effects, and recommended emergency procedures.

Other issued warnings are:

- Small-craft warnings. When a hurricane moves within a few hundred miles of the coast, advisories warn small-craft operators to take precautions and not to venture into the open ocean.
- Gale warnings. When winds of 38–55 miles per hour (33–48 knots) are expected, a gale warning is added to the advisory message.
- Storm warnings. When winds of 55–74 miles per hour (48–64 knots) are expected, a storm warning is added to the advisory message.

Gale and storm warning messages describe the coastal area that should be affected, the time when the warning will apply, and the expected intensity of the disturbance. *When storm warnings are part of a tropical cyclone advisory, they may change to hurricane warnings if the storm continues along the coast.* Radio and television stations will broadcast the latest hurricane advisories.

When a Hurricane Warning Is Announced

- Keep your radio or television on and listen for the latest Weather Service warnings and advisories. When a hurricane approaches, also listen for *tornado* watches and warnings. (See "Suggested Procedures" for tornadoes, page 21.) If power fails, use a portable battery radio or your car radio. Check your battery-powered equipment. Your radio may be your only link with the world outside the hurricane, and emergency cooking facilities and flashlights will be essential if utility services are interrupted.

- Plan your time before the storm arrives. Waiting until the "last minute" might mean you'll be marooned or unprepared.
- Leave beaches or other low-lying areas that may be swept by high tides. Leave early; don't run the risk of being marooned.
- Moor your boat securely before the storm arrives, or move it to a designated safe area. When your boat is moored, leave it, and don't return once the wind and waves are up.
- Board up windows or protect them with storm shutters or tape. Danger to small windows is mainly from wind-driven debris. Larger windows may be broken by wind pressure.
- Secure outdoor objects that might be blown away or uprooted. Garbage cans, garden tools, toys, signs, porch furniture, and other normally harmless items become missiles of destruction in hurricane winds. Anchor them or store them inside before the storm strikes.
- Store drinking water in clean, closed containers such as jugs, bottles, and cooking utensils. Your town's water supply may be contaminated by flooding or damaged by the hurricane.
- Keep your car fueled. Service stations may be inoperable for several days after the storm strikes because of flooding or interrupted electrical power.

Evacuation

If you are warned to evacuate your home temporarily and move to another location (including predesignated hurricane shelters), there are certain things to remember and do. Here are the most important ones:

- Follow the instructions and advice of local authorities. If you are told to evacuate, do so promptly. If you are instructed to move to a certain location, go there—don't go anywhere else. If certain travel routes are specified or recommended, use those routes rather than trying to find shortcuts of your own. If you are told to shut off your water, gas, or electric service before leaving home, do so. Also find out from the radio or television where emergency housing and food supply facilities are located, in case you need to use them.

- Secure your home before leaving. If you have time, and if you have not received other instructions from local authorities, you should lock your house doors and windows. Park your car in the garage, carport, or driveway, close windows, and lock the car (unless you are driving to your new temporary location).
- Travel with care. If local authorities are arranging transportation for you, precautions will be taken for your safety. But if you are walking or driving your own car to another location, keep in mind these things: (1) leave early enough so as not to be marooned by flooded roads, fallen trees, and wires; (2) make sure you have enough gasoline in your car; (3) follow recommended routes; and (4) keep listening to the radio for additional information and instructions from your local government.

During a Hurricane

- Unless advised to evacuate, stay at home if your house is sturdy and on high ground. If it is not, or if you live in a mobile home, move to a designated shelter and stay there until the storm is over. Mobile homes are especially vulnerable to overturning during strong winds. Damage can be minimized by securing mobile homes with heavy cables anchored in concrete footings.
- Remain indoors during the hurricane. Travel is extremely dangerous when winds and tides are whipping through your area.
- Beware of the eye of the hurricane. If the calm storm center passes directly overhead, there will be a lull in the wind lasting from a few minutes to half an hour or more. Stay in a safe place unless emergency repairs are absolutely necessary. Remember, at the other side of the eye, the winds rise very rapidly to hurricane force, and come from the opposite direction.

After a Hurricane Passes

- Remain in shelters until informed by those in charge that you may return to your home.
- Use extreme caution when entering or working in buildings damaged or weakened by the disaster; they may collapse without warning. Also, live electrical circuits may be exposed.
- Don't take lanterns, torches, or lighted cigarettes into buildings damaged by a hurricane; there may be leaking gas lines or

flammable material. Use a battery-powered flashlight or spotlight.

- Stay away from fallen or damaged electric wires. Notify the power company or the police or fire department.
- Check for leaking gas pipes in your home. Do this by smell— *don't* use matches or candles. If you smell gas, do this: (1) open all windows and doors; (2) leave the house immediately; (3) turn off the main gas valve at the meter; (4) notify the gas company or the police; (5) don't reenter the house until you are told it is safe to do so.
- Report broken sewer or water mains to the water department.
- If any of your electrical appliances are wet, first turn off the main power switch in your house, then unplug the wet appliance, dry it out, reconnect it, and finally, turn on the main power switch. (Caution: Don't do any of these things while you are wet or standing in water.) If fuses blow when the electric power is restored, turn off the main power switch and inspect for short circuits in your home wiring, appliances, and equipment.
- Check your food and water supplies before using them. Foods that require refrigeration may be spoiled if electric power has been off for some time. Also, do not use fresh food that has been in contact with floodwaters.
- Don't drive unless necessary; but if you must, drive with caution. Watch for hazards to yourself and others, and report them to local police or fire departments.
- Stay away from disaster areas. Sightseeing could interfere with first-aid or rescue work, and may be dangerous as well.
- Keep tuned to your radio or television stations for instructions from your local government on where to obtain necessary medical care and emergency assistance for housing, clothing, and food, and how to help yourself and your community recover from the emergency.
- *Remember*: Hurricanes moving inland can cause severe flooding. Stay away from river banks and streams until all potential flooding is past.

Note

1. U.S. Department of Commerce, National Oceanic and Atmospheric Administration (NOAA), *Hurricane—The Greatest Storm on Earth* (Washington, D.C.: U.S. Government Printing Office, 1971), p. 12.

5. FOREST, BRUSH, AND GRASS FIRES

Man is responsible for 65 percent of the 30,000 forest, brush, and grass fires that occur annually throughout the United States. Arsonists and debris burners are responsible for about 21 and 16 percent, respectively. Lightning, which accounts for about 35 percent of the fires over the entire United States, is the leading cause of forest fires in the western part of the country.

In the United States, which has a total area in excess of 2 billion acres, more than half is in forest and grassland. The remaining area consists of 500 million acres of cities, highways, and water areas and some 500 million acres of farmlands and small wooded lots, usually lying outside of city limits.

Fuels in the woodlands are varied in kind, quality, amount, and degree of flammability. As the deciduous trees lose their leaves in the fall of the year, ample ground fuel is provided for serious fires, until winter conditions make the fuel less flammable. One of the greatest dangers occurs in the spring, when the leafless trees allow the full sweep of drying winds. In coniferous forests the accumulation of needle fuels is a gradual process; but when dry, these fuels can produce an almost explosive force. The hazardous combination of fuels, weather, and people can quickly transform a static area to one of dynamic fire.

Loss of life, although not usually as high as in other disasters, is a too-frequent tragedy in most fire disasters. Many businesses are forced to cease operations, communications and electrical power systems are disrupted, and the losses in recreation and travel activities are incalculable. Private residences are often destroyed in forest and brush fires. Of national significance is the complete destruction of valuable resources such as timber, grass, wildlife habitat, and scenic vistas.

The greatest single fire disaster this country has ever known, in terms of lives and property lost, occurred in eastern Wisconsin in 1871. The Peshtigo fire burned over 1¼ million acres and killed 1,500 people.

Burned-over area. *Courtesy U.S. Forest Service, USDA.*

Forest fires destroy wildlife. *Courtesy U.S. Forest Service, USDA.*

36

The Tillamook Burn fire in Oregon in 1933 destroyed as much timber (10.5 billion board feet) as had been cut in the entire United States during the previous year. Some 300,000 acres, mostly virgin timber, were devastated.

In the Maine fire in 1941, which burned over 200,000 acres, 15 lives were lost, more than 1,200 homes were destroyed, and property loss was estimated at $30 million.

Real estate and residential losses run high when rural forest and grass fires reach the conflagration stage and invade urban areas. With the continuing migration of people and the extension of urban and suburban areas into woodlands and grassland fringes, the chances of a conflagration with major losses are increasing significantly. In Southern California during a one-month period of critical fire weather in 1970, 1,260 fires burned more than 600,000 acres, killing 14 people, destroying some 900 homes and other structures, and creating a potential for an aftermath of erosion, floods, and mudslides.

Kinds of Fire

Conflagrations may be described as forest, brush, or grass fires—although any single disaster may involve more than one of these kinds of fire. Woodland blazes are further characterized as surface, duff, crown, spot, or tree fires.

Forest Fire

- The surface fire is the most common in eastern woodlands. It usually runs through the flash fuels that litter the forest floor. The surface is generally fast burning and hot and is easily influenced by wind action. Normally, however, it is fairly easy to control.
- The duff fire, or underground fire, is usually the result of a surface fire. Most duff fires occur during prolonged dry spells, burning deep into the accumulated leaf litter or peat called "duff" and smoldering to a depth of several feet. The burning is slow, but the intense heat dries out the fuel in its path, enabling the duff fire to burn into areas normally too damp to support combustion. A duff fire may smolder for days with little show of smoke or flames, and for this reason it is particularly dangerous. The fire is also difficult to extinguish: it must be dug out, trenched down to mineral soil, or flooded out with water.

- The crown fire occurs when fire sweeps through the foliage of trees and large bushes. Crown fires are supported only by the fuel burning on the surface of the plant. Generally they are controlled by separating the fuel from the fire or by attacking the fire where the amount of surface fuel is not sufficient to support a crown fire.
- Spot fires are nearly always caused by sparks or embers carried ahead of a large moving fire to where they ignite new fires. These small "spots" may burn until they join together or are overrun by the larger fire. They are particularly dangerous, because they can sometimes jump as far as a mile in advance of a parent fire, crossing firebreaks that firefighters have dug to contain the blaze.
- Tree fires (i.e., fires inside trees) are fairly common in most states and are usually detected and extinguished before they have time to spread to the surface. These fires may be caused by lightning or by people smoking out bees or game. If a tree fire is too far advanced, the tree is usually felled and the fire extinguished with dirt or water. Otherwise, water from a spray tank is used to put out the fire.

Brush Fire

A typical example is the chaparral fire that rages periodically in California. Chaparral, a dry fuel, is composed of chamise, manganite, and scrub oak—flash fuels that offer easy ignition and are consumed rapidly and completely. Brush fires are difficult to control because they generate intense heat and consume available ground fuels very quickly.

Grass Fire

This type of fire is most dangerous when the grass is in a dried or "cured" state. Although grass can grow to heights in excess of six feet, it still has the burning behavior of a flash ground fuel. Heavy grass fuel burning ahead of a high wind can become a dangerous menace because of its heat, speed of travel, and power to roll over barriers.

The Threat of Forest, Brush, and Grass Fires

In the East, the normal fire seasons are spring and fall, while severe weather conditions may cause them to extend through the summer and winter months. In the West, the normal fire-danger period develops during the dry summer months. This whole pat-

Brush fire. *Courtesy U.S. Forest Service, USDA.*

tern can be materially altered by changes in weather and forest fuels and by the care or carelessness of man. A drought or a prolonged dry spell threatens a continuous fire potential until sufficient precipitation occurs.

Because of the variety and changing condition of fuels, the degree of flammability will tend to fluctuate. Four weather conditions—precipitation, relative humidity, temperature, and winds—influence forest and grass fire behavior, chiefly because of their effect upon fuels. Topography has a decided effect upon fire behavior in that fire burns more intensely and rapidly uphill because uphill drafts fan the flame. This advancing flow of heat also more quickly heats and ignites the materials above the flames.

Suggested Procedures

Forest, brush, and grass fires can occur at any time of the year but mostly occur during long, dry hot spells. The majority of these fires are caused by human carelessness or ignorance. Fire prevention, therefore, is mainly a matter of understanding the importance of grasslands and forests, recognizing the danger of fire in the woods and on the plains, and assuming personal responsibility for the protection of our national resources.

When a Forest, Brush, or Grass Fire Threatens

Although forest, brush, and grass fires can start without warning, federal and state governments maintain a system of watchtowers and surveillance aircraft manned by the U.S. Forest Service and state forest services to ensure that fires can be detected, warnings issued, and necessary emergency action taken.

Knowing what to do when a fire threatens may mean the difference between life and death. To help you prepare for the possibility of fires in your area, the following procedures are suggested:

- If you see a fire, report it immediately by phone to the local police department, fire department, or fire warden. Do *not* use the phone to get information. For that, depend on your radio or television.
- Keep posted on the progress of the fire by listening to radio and television broadcasts.
- Put out all fires in the home and other structures. If you are burning debris for cleanup, such as "woods-burning" in the South, stop immediately. If in the woods, put out campfires.

- Make certain your own property is clear of combustibles, particularly brush that is hazardous to your home or other structures. If necessary, and if time permits, remove and clear away flammable vegetation up to 30 feet on each side of your home or other structure.
- Hook up garden hoses and check out your water supply for possible "wetting down" of roofs if sparks threaten.
- Close all windows (cover them if possible); remove combustibles near windows and other openings; protect and secure stock and pet animals.
- After your own home is prepared, be ready to assist in constructing community firebreaks *if* asked to do so.
- If area evacuation is called for, get full information on exit routes and relocation areas.

If Your Community Is Involved in a Forest, Brush, or Grass Fire

- Cooperate with authorities. Keep posted on the progress of the fire by listening to radio and television broadcasts.
- Follow evacuation directions.
- *Do not use or block firefighting entrance routes.* These are reserved for emergency services only.
- Assist in community firefighting if you are between the stipulated ages and able-bodied. All others keep clear of fire area.
- Make certain you are under the supervision of a designated firefighter. Follow his instructions; he knows how the fire is being fought and where you will be of most value to the operation.
- Follow safety precautions to prevent getting trapped. Ground winds and fuels are tricky. Follow instructions. Keep informed. Know where the fire is. Know your escape route. Keep calm. Maintain communication with your supervisor. (*Don't go it alone!*) Make sure you understand instructions.

Earthquake damage. *Courtesy U.S. Army.*

6. EARTHQUAKES

We tend to think of our earth as "solid ground," but its crust is really a series of plates edged against each other, the whole resting like a cracked egg shell on a liquid core of molten and semi-molten magma. From the beginning of time great forces and pressures within the earth have constantly broken, folded, and moved these plates about.

The theory of "plate tectonics," as a cause of earthquakes, has gained wide acceptance in the past several years. The strongest evidence of its validity is the existence of earthquake *belts*, which outline the large plates and provide a measure of movement where the plates join. As the plates shift, stresses build up, until the plates fracture or slip. This release of stress is called an earthquake. It is much as though you were to place a strip of glass across your knee and apply gradual pressure to both ends. It flexes so far, then fractures with a sudden release of energy that leaves the two ends vibrating in your hands.

The small area of the crust where the stresses are relieved is the focus of an earthquake. From this point, vibrations or "waves" radiate in all directions through the body of the earth. When the vibrations arrive at the surface of the earth, sometimes from as deep as 700 kilometers, they create secondary surface waves. The frequency and strength of these secondary waves determine the severity of the earthquake.

The duration of most earthquake tremors is expressed in seconds. For example, the 1933 Long Beach, California, earthquake lasted seven seconds, whereas the 1906 quake in San Francisco extended over forty seconds.

An Earthquake in Motion

A large earthquake is one of nature's most devastating phenomena. The energy released by an earthquake of 8.5 magnitude on the Richter scale is equivalent to 12,000 times the energy released by the Hiroshima atomic bomb. While these cataclysms have their foci well below the earth's surface, cities have been destroyed and thousands of lives lost in a few seconds as a result of great earthquakes of the past.

The onset of a large earthquake is initially signaled by a deep rumbling or by disturbed air making a rushing sound, followed by a series of violent motions in the ground. The surroundings seem to disintegrate. Often the ground cracks open, and there can be large permanent displacements—21 feet horizontally in San Francisco in 1906, and 47 feet vertically at Yakutat Bay, Alaska, in 1899. Buildings, bridges, dams, tunnels, and other rigid structures are sheared in two or collapse when subjected to this movement. Vibrations are sometimes so severe that large trees are snapped off or uprooted. People standing have been knocked down and their legs broken by the sudden lateral accelerations.

Buildings, somewhat like tuning forks, usually respond to particular frequencies of vibration that set them in motion, swaying and quivering. Sometimes resonant motion results. This is particularly destructive, because the strength of the vibrations increases (theoretically without limits), and usually structural failure occurs. Adjacent buildings can vibrate out of phase and pound each other to pieces. Water tanks, bridges, and the walls of high-rise buildings are especially vulnerable to the vibrations. The walls of high-rise buildings without adequate lateral bracing frequently fall outward, allowing the floors to cascade one on top of the other, crushing the occupants. In poorer countries, where mud brick and adobe are used extensively in construction, collapse is often total—even to the point of returning the bricks to dust.

Water in tanks, ponds, and rivers is frequently thrown from its confines. In lakes, an oscillation known as "seiching" occurs, in which the water surges from one end to the other, reaching great heights and overflowing the banks. During the 1964 earthquake in Alaska, for example, water at Memphis, Tennessee—5,000 miles from the earthquake's center—rose six feet as a result of seiching.

Fire damage frequently increases because fire-fighting equipment is destroyed and water mains are ruptured. This secondary effect is well illustrated by the San Francisco earthquake of 1906. Only about 20 percent of the half billion dollars in damage is thought to have been caused by the earthquake directly; the remainder was caused by fire, which was out of control for several days. One of the greatest disasters of all time, the Kwanto, Japan, earthquake in 1923, also resulted in enormous fire losses. Almost 40 percent of the dead perished in a firestorm that engulfed an open area where people had gathered in a futile attempt to escape the conflagration.

Other effects include the disruption of electric power and gas service, which further contributes to fire damage. Also, highways and rail systems are frequently put out of service, presenting special difficulties to rescue and relief workers.

Tsunamis (seismic sea waves) are also frequent secondary effects of earthquakes. They are a unique phenomenon, however, and are treated in another chapter.

A Worldwide Threat

Several million earthquakes occur annually throughout the world. They range from barely perceptible tremors to catastrophic shocks. Most earthquakes originate beneath the sea, where they cause little concern—unless they create tsunamis. Such waves occasionally cause damage and loss of life thousands of miles away, as well as near the earthquake's origin. Approximately 700 shocks each year may be classed as strong—that is, capable of causing considerable damage where they occur (Richter scale magnitude of 5.5 or greater). The National Earthquake Information Center, in cooperation with foreign and domestic agencies,

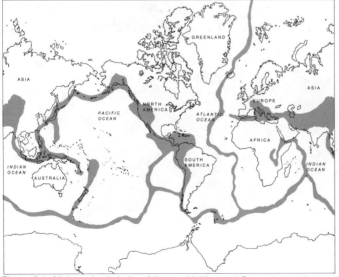

Figure 6-1. Major seismic belts of the world. *National Oceanic and Atmospheric Administration.*

45

locates the larger shocks and produces maps pinpointing earthquake locations. These maps depict well-defined seismic belts stretching over large areas of the world.

Earthquakes in these well-defined belts are to be expected; but great shocks also occur occasionally outside the belts—for example, in southeastern Missouri and the Charleston, South Carolina, area—though many years usually elapse between destructive shocks in these regions. The cities of the Pacific coast are therefore not alone in their vulnerability to earthquakes, for the threat also exists in many areas ordinarily considered only moderately seismic. As a matter of fact, there is seismic activity in all regions of the United States.

Earthquake-prone areas include some of the most densely populated regions of the world, such as Japan, the western United States, and the shores of the Mediterranean Sea. It is estimated that more than 500 million people could well suffer property damage and that a significant proportion of them are in danger of losing their lives in severe earthquakes. In areas of the world where minimum control of construction and design is exercised, death tolls often reach staggering numbers.

The areas of heaviest activity are known and well defined, but it is not yet possible to predict when an earthquake will occur in a given area. However, a seismic risk map for the United States has been developed. (see Figure 6-2.)

Figure 6-2. Seismic risk map of the United States. *U.S. Geological Survey.*

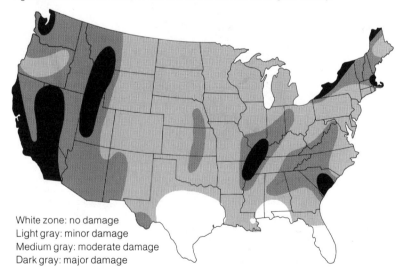

White zone: no damage
Light gray: minor damage
Medium gray: moderate damage
Dark gray: major damage

The loss of life in the United States has been relatively light, considering the number of destructive earthquakes that have occurred. This is explained partially by better-than-usual construction practices, but more by fortuitous circumstances, such as the majority of the people being in relatively safe places at the time of earthquakes. For example, the loss of life in the 1971 San Fernando, California, quake would have been much greater had it occurred when the freeways were crowded with the normal rush-hour traffic.

Property loss has involved damage to highways, waterways, transmission lines, sewers and underground pipelines, and railways. Sometimes land itself is lost through subsidence of large areas, erosion, and slide action.

In many areas, construction standards are low and casualty rates are correspondingly high. However, modern structures and even construction designed specifically to resist earthquakes (such as in Caracas, Venezuela, and San Fernando, California) often suffer irreparable damage or complete destruction.

In the United States and a few other countries, various agencies have gone to great lengths to make the public aware of the need for proper construction and to instruct them in the proper actions to be taken during and after an earthquake—all this in the hope that this knowledge will lessen the vulnerability of people and property to earthquakes.

Suggested Procedures

The actual earth movement of an earthquake is seldom a direct cause of death or injury. However, this movement causes the collapse of buildings and other structures. Most casualties result from (1) falling bricks and plaster; (2) splintering glass; (3) toppling furniture, collapsing walls, falling pictures and mirrors; (4) rock slides on mountains and hillsides; (5) fallen power lines; (6) sea waves generated by earthquakes; and (7) fire caused by broken gas lines and spillage of gasoline and other flammables. With the foregoing in mind, the following procedures are suggested for before, during, and after an earthquake.

Before an Earthquake

■ Check for earthquake hazards. Bolt down or provide other strong support for water heaters and other gas appliances. Place large and heavy objects on the lower shelves of closets and storage areas. Brace or anchor high or top-heavy objects. Wire or anchor overhead fixtures. Do not stack glassware or crystal.

- Keep an emergency supply of food which requires little cooking and no refrigeration; electric and gas power may be interrupted.
- Keep a portable radio, emergency cooking equipment, and flashlights in good working order.
- Keep first-aid and critical medical supplies (prescription drugs, insulin, etc.) at hand.
- In new construction, follow building codes or other sound practices to reduce earthquake hazards. Build on solid ground or dig down to bedrock when laying foundations. Avoid earth fill and sedimentary areas as much as possible, and do not build below dams that might be damaged.

During an Earthquake

- Remain calm. Think through the consequences of any action you plan to take. Try to reassure others.
- If you are indoors, watch for falling plaster, bricks, light fixtures, and other objects. Watch out for high bookcases, china cabinets, shelves, and other furniture that might slide or topple. Stay away from windows, mirrors, and chimneys. If in danger, get under a table, desk, or bed, in a corner away from windows, or in a strong doorway. Encourage others to follow your example.
- Do not run outside.
- Don't use candles, matches, or other open flames during the tremor. Douse all fires.
- If you're outside, avoid high buildings, walls, power poles, and other objects that could fall. Do not run through the streets. If surrounded by buildings, take shelter in the nearest strong one. If possible, however, move to an open area away from all hazards.
- If you are in an automobile, stop in the safest place available, preferably an open area. Stop as quickly as safety permits, but stay in the vehicle for the shelter it offers.

After an Earthquake

- Check for injuries. Do not attempt to move seriously injured person unless they are in immediate danger of further injury.
- Check for fires.

- Wear shoes near debris or broken glass.
- Check utility lines and appliances for damage. If gas leaks exist, shut off the main gas valve. Shut off electrical power if there is damage to wiring. Do not use matches or lighters until it has been established that there are no gas leaks. Furthermore, do not turn light switches on and off. This creates sparks that can ignite gas from broken lines.
- Clean up spilled medicines, drugs, and other potentially harmful materials immediately.
- Draw a moderate quantity of water in case service should be disrupted. Do not draw a large quantity: this could interfere with firefighting. If water is off, emergency water may be obtained from hot-water heaters, toilet tanks, melted ice cubes, and water packed in canned vegetables. If water pipes are damaged, shut off water supply at the main valve.
- Check to see that sewage lines are intact before permitting continued flushing of toilets.
- Do not eat or drink anything from open containers near shattered glass. Such liquids may be strained through many folds of a clean handkerchief or cloth but only if their use is essential.
- Check chimneys for cracks and damages; unnoticed damage could lead to a fire. The initial check should be made from a distance. Approach chimneys with great caution.
- Check closets and storage areas. Open closet and cupboard doors carefully to guard against having objects fall on you.
- Check your house or apartment building for structural damage; if you deem it necessary, evacuate your family until an authority declares it safe to return. Stay out of severely damaged buildings; aftershocks can shake them down.
- Do not heed or spread rumors. They often do great harm following disasters. Stay off the telephone, except to report an emergency. Turn on your radio and/or television to get the latest emergency bulletins.
- Do not go sightseeing, particularly in beach and waterfront areas where sea waves could strike, or in areas where buildings have collapsed or where electrical wires may be down but still alive. Keep the streets clear for passage of emergency vehicles.
- Be prepared for additional earthquake shocks.
- Respond to requests for assistance from police, firefighting, and relief organizations, but do not go into damaged areas unless your assistance has been requested.

Tsunami damage. *Courtesy Wide World Photos.*

7. TSUNAMIS

A tsunami (pronounced soo-'nah-mee) is a train of ocean waves created by disturbances—usually earthquakes—in the ocean floor. (The term *tidal wave* is sometimes used, but this is inaccurate, because tsunamis have almost nothing to do with tides.)

Tsunami waves are enormously destructive to life and property and have been responsible for some of the worst disasters in history. The tsunami caused by the explosion of the volcanic island Krakatoa in 1883 sent 100-foot waves roaring into Java and Sumatra, drowning 36,500 people. Another struck Japan in 1896, killing 27,000.

Tsunamis generally occur only in and around the Pacific Ocean. Since 1900, more than 180 tsunamis have been recorded in the Pacific. Of these, 34 caused damage near the source only, and 9 were destructive both locally and distantly. Japan is the most frequent victim (hence our use of the Japanese word for "harbor wave" to describe this killer); but other areas such as the Aleutian Islands, Hawaii, and Chile are especially susceptible. Historically, a tsunami of major proportions has struck the United States or its Pacific possessions on the average of once every eight years.

Local waves generated by earthquake action on water in confined areas are sometimes called tsunamis but do not have their true characteristics. They can, however, be very destructive and reach great heights.

The Anatomy of a Tsunami

Perhaps it is because tsunamis are a relatively rare phenomenon that they are neither completely understood by scientists nor fully appreciated by the inhabitants of vulnerable coastlines.

A tsunami is unique in the amount of energy it contains. The energy of earthquakes that generate tsunamis (7.5 or higher on the Richter scale) can be several times greater than that of the largest nuclear explosions. The waves themselves are believed to originate as vertically displaced columns of ocean water. Once generated, they speed silently across the open sea at velocities approaching 600 miles an hour. The wave may be only 2 feet high in mid-ocean, but its tremendous energy is revealed in the long period between crests—from 15 minutes to 2 hours. When the waves enter shallow water along a coast, they are slowed to less than 40 miles an hour. As a result, much of their energy is converted to wave height—the tsunami waves become roaring monsters of 100 feet or more.

Tsunamis maintain their great strength for very long distances. They may strike in the immediate vicinity of an earthquake or on the opposite shore of the Pacific. The Krakatoa eruption in 1883 produced a tsunami whose waves traveled two or three times around the globe.

It is impossible to say with any certainty what size a tsunami will assume at specific locations or how it will accomplish its destructive work. This is because shoal conditions and coastal topography vary widely, even within relatively small coastal regions. Thus, a wave five feet high at one beach area may be 50 feet high not far away. Furthermore, a tsunami is not a single wave, but a series of large waves; and usually the third or fourth wave is the largest. Throughout a tsunami the time interval between crests tends to remain large—perhaps several minutes—and sometimes the first thing that happens is not a wave, but a mysterious withdrawing of the sea that leaves fish flopping on bare sand—followed by a huge wave that often traps the unwary.

When a tsunami struck Hilo, Hawaii, in May 1960, eyewitnesses watched waves break over the tops of warehouses. And in Lituya Bay, Alaska, on July 9, 1958, a colossal tsunami wave—perhaps the highest wave ever known to man—sloshed an astonishing 1,600 feet up a mountainside.

The Destructive Power of Tsunamis

Our understanding of the physics of tsunamis may be limited; our knowledge of their destructive potential is not. Of all the secondary disasters that an earthquake can generate—landslides, avalanches, flooding, fires, etc.—the tsunami can be the greatest hazard. In fact, the destructive power of a tsunami can rival that of the originating earthquake itself. Tsunamis, major and local, took the most lives in the Alaskan earthquake of 1964. In 1960, the people of Hilo, Hawaii, suffered 61 dead and 282 injured from a tsunami of distant origin, an earthquake in Chile.

Current standards tentatively define hazard areas on Pacific coasts as follows: areas within one mile of the coast and lower than 50 feet above sea level are danger areas for tsunamis of distant origin; and areas within one mile of the coast and lower than 100 feet above sea level are danger areas for tsunamis of local origin.[1]

A tsunami unleashes its maximum destructive force at the water's edge. However, damage farther inland is potentially high because of the floating debris that batters inland installations, even though the force of the wave has diminished. Ships moored in harbors are often swamped and sunk or left battered and stranded high on the shore. Breakwaters and piers collapse, sometimes because of scouring actions that sweep away their foundations and sometimes because of the sheer impact of the waves. Railroad yards and oil tank farms near the waterfront are particularly vulnerable, and oil fires frequently result and are spread by the waves.

Tsunamis cause such devastation that the affected areas are generally left devoid of all housing and vital services. Port facilities, fishing fleets, and public utilities are frequently the backbone of the economy of the affected areas, and these are the very resources which generally receive the most severe damage. Until debris can be cleared, wharves and piers rebuilt, railroad yards and tank farms reestablished, utilities repaired, and fishing fleets restored, communities may find themselves without fuel, food, and employment. Wherever water transport is a vital means of supply, disruption of coastal systems can have far-reaching economic effects.

Suggested Procedures

The forces involved in a tsunami cannot be controlled. The most that can be accomplished, therefore, is to reduce the hazard prior to its onslaught.

Long-term measures include urban planning and zoning to exclude high-use public facilities and vital industrial complexes from vulnerable areas.

Early warning and well-organized evacuation procedures are the best short-term measures. If warning is received early enough (2 to 5 hours), people can be evacuated, ships can clear harbors, and seek a safer anchorage, planes, trucks, and railroad cars can be moved, and buildings can be closed, shuttered, and sand-bagged.

The National Weather Service issues tsunami watches and warnings.

A *tsunami watch* is an alert to *possible* danger and is issued when an earthquake big enough and in the right place to cause a tsunami has been detected by seismograph stations.

A *tsunami warning,* an alert to *actual* danger, is issued when recording stations nearest the earthquake report the presence of seismic sea waves, indicating that a tsunami has been generated.

A tsunami warning gives the estimated time of arrival (accurate to about 2 minutes per hour of warning) of the first wave of the tsunami at any of some 50 locations throughout the Pacific. However, because the same tsunami may be vastly different at different points on the shore, a warning does not carry estimates of how high the water will rise. Tsunamis of any magnitude should be accorded the utmost respect.

Before a Tsunami

- Keep a small emergency supply of food that can be quickly moved to your automobile.
- Not all earthquakes cause tsunamis, but many do. A strong earthquake felt in a low-lying coastal area is a natural warning of possible, immediate danger. When you hear that an earth-quake has occurred, stand by for a tsunami emergency.
- Approaching tsunamis are sometimes heralded by an unusual rise or fall of coastal water. This is nature's tsunami warning; pay strict heed to it, especially if you are in a beach or water-front area.

When a Tsunami Watch Is Announced

- No matter what the hour of the day or night, stay tuned to a radio or television station for further information—at least until you are notified that the danger is over.
- Make sure your car is fueled. If a warning is issued and evac-uation is to be by automobile, yours will do you no good if it runs out of gas halfway to safety.
- Ensure that necessary medications (prescription drugs, insulin, etc.) are at hand.

When a Tsunami Warning is Issued

- Cooperate fully with local Civil Defense, police, and other emergency organizations. When you are told to evacuate, do so without delay. *Above all,* get to higher ground before the tsunami overtakes you.
- If you want to take valuables with you, take only those that can be moved quickly and easily, and only if time permits. Don't risk your life to save material possessions.
- *If* time permits, turn off main gas valves, water valves, and electrical power in your home.
- Paradoxically, the very warning that can sometimes save lives can also lure the curious to watch an event as spectacular as a tsunami. *Never* go down to the beach to watch for a tsunami. When you can see the waves, you are too close to escape them.

After a Tsunami

- A tsunami is not a single wave, but a series of waves. Stay out of danger areas until an "all-clear" is issued by competent authority. In the tsunamis of May 1960, the third and fourth waves striking the Chilean coast were higher than the first or second in some places. Many people died because they returned to the coast too early.
- Never enter a disaster area to sightsee. Your presence can impede cleanup, rescue, and repair operations.
- Beware of fire hazards from downed electrical lines, broken gas lines, and the like. Reenter buildings only when they have been certified safe.

Note

1. Coast and Geodetic Survey, 1965.

Landslide damage. *Courtesy U.S. Geological Survey.*

Landslide caused by earthquake. *Courtesy U.S. Geological Survey.*

8. LANDSLIDE

The danger of landslides is ever present in all mountainous countries, such as northern Italy, Switzerland, Norway, Nepal, Tibet,
and the countries of the Andes in South America.

The United States was until recently considered less susceptible to disasters from landslides, because most of its mountainous areas are not heavily populated. However, growth in populated areas has begun to push steadily into marginal areas, where
land development not only encounters existing landslide hazards
but also creates totally new hazards.

In the Los Angeles basin, for example, the foothills of the San
Gabriel and Santa Monica mountains, once considered stark wilderness, are now blanketed by residential development. Thousands of expensive homes perch precariously on the hillsides. In
the course of construction, stable slopes have been scarred. And
the presence of more people has increased the danger of brush
fires, which frequently strip the hillsides of moisture-retaining vegetation. Therefore, when a subtropical storm dumped 10 inches
of rain on Southern California during January 18–26, 1969, immense landslides took 95 lives and caused damage totaling $138
million—all this in an area where, 20 years previously, the damage
would have been negligible.

Causes of Landslides

Landslides can be categorized according to their causes, as follows:

Slow Erosion

Water (flowing, freezing, and thawing) and wind erosion gradually
wear away supporting materials and cause two types of slides:
rock falls, where overhanging material drops to the valley floor
without disturbing material in between; and avalanches, where
dry material sweeps down a mountainside, gathering momentum
and masses of loose debris as it progresses.

Water

Heavy rains frequently cause marginally stable slopes to give way to two forms of slides: avalanches, which sweep away surface material below the main failure zone; and mud flows or slumps, in which soil liquefies and flows downward, usually from a tilted basin-shaped area, leaving a scarped depression at the upper end and an outflow over the surface below, where it comes to rest.

Often, slopes stabilized by vegetation are denuded by forest or brush fires. The scarred areas lose their capacity for holding moisture and, during the following rainy season, the rainfall can turn those slopes into rivers of mud.

Glacial Action

Advancing glaciers frequently displace the material supporting valley walls. Then, when the glaciers melt, the results are landslides and mud flows—the latter particularly common in stream deltas.

Earthquakes

Earthquakes cause landslides of two types. In one type, material is shaken loose and forms an avalanche, as in the Hebgen, Montana, earthquake in 1959. In the other type, the particles of the soil act as a liquid, causing slumping and ground failure over wide areas, as at the Van Norman Dam following the San Fernando, California, earthquake in 1971. This effect is evident even in level terrain, where buildings actually sink into the ground. During the 1964 Alaska earthquake, destruction in the Turnagain Arm area of Anchorage brought the soil-liquefaction problem forcefully to the attention of engineers and the general public. Similar conditions exist in other metropolitan areas, such as the cities around San Francisco Bay and Puget Sound, where many buildings rest on water-soaked landfill or relatively unstable clay slopes.

Engineering Defects

In some instances, man-made highways and railroad cuts or embankments traverse the toe of a slide area, in which case the up-slope material becomes unstable and susceptible to slides. This situation also occurs in excavations for dams, bridge abutments, and buildings. If the slope stability has been miscalculated, erosion or heavy rains can trigger very destructive slides.

Devastating Effects

In actuality, landslides often result from a combination of the causes described above, and they often combine several types of slide action. Landslides involve great amounts of material which move with tremendous force and often at startling velocity. Everything in the path of a large slide is destroyed. Where soil liquefaction occurs, bizarre effects are encountered. On relatively gradual slopes, foundation material can lose its bearing strength and an entire subdivision or village may shift downslope; deep cuts and depressions are often formed, and buildings are tilted and torn asunder, or they settle into the ground.

People living on sloping ground, especially in mountain valleys that have heavy snow or rainfall, are vulnerable to landslides. The danger is greater if the area also has a history of seismic activity. And people who live on seacoast plateaus in seismic areas are also very much exposed to the danger of mud flows and ground liquefaction.

Slope, precipitation, and geologic conditions are the primary factors considered in identifying landslide risk. Available data indicate that slides are not common on slopes of less than 5 degrees or more than 35 degrees, or where mean annual precipitation is less than 10 inches. A historical summary of landslides in the United States is presented in Table 8-1.

Suggested Procedures

Property located on a slide area or in its path cannot be protected from the destructive forces of a landslide, particularly one caused by an earthquake. Such slides occur infrequently in populated areas, but when they do, they are even more destructive to property situated in their limited path than are tsunamis. The best procedure, therefore, is to take advantage of the few precautionary measures that can be taken *before* a landslide occurs.

To Prevent Landslide Damage

- Be very careful when choosing building sites. Think very carefully before you build on a hillside or in a ravine. A building site can be test-bored and its normal slide quotient can be calculated. But no one can foretell a property's slide rating under abnormal conditions like torrential rains, rapid thaw of heavy snowpack, destruction of vegetation by fire or land clearance, or weather erosion.

- Before buying or renting a house or apartment, check basements for cracked walls and floors. Inspect the neighborhood for displaced street slabs, fractured retaining walls, tilted power and telephone poles—all clues to earth movement.
- Sometimes carefully engineered drainage systems can minimize the saturation of soils during heavy rainfall. If you already live in a hillside area, it may be wise to use whatever influence you have to persuade local governments to consider installing these protective systems.
- When camping, avoid campgrounds in deep ravines or under sheer cliffs. Think twice about camping below any kind of slope, especially those that ooze moisture or lack vegetation.
- Wherever you are, keep alert for signs of mudslides; unless there is an earthquake or explosion (which can start a dry earth slide), you normally won't encounter earthslides except during or after rain. Be prepared to flee at an instant's notice.
- Occasionally local officials will order the evacuation of an area where it appears that mud flows or other slides are imminent. Cooperate fully and quickly when such warnings are issued.

During a Slide

- If you see or hear a slide coming, the only thing worth doing is to run. Run laterally on the hillside, or at an angle slightly downhill; don't run directly downhill in the path of the slide. It may be possible to shout warnings to others as you flee.

After a Slide

- Never rush into an area where a slide has occurred; keep in mind the possibility of recurring slides that could well overtake you.
- Cooperate fully with organized rescue efforts. Work only under expert supervision, and be extremely careful when working around collapsed buildings and debris.
- Beware of the dangers of broken gas lines and damaged electrical circuits.

TABLE 8-1. LANDSLIDES OF THE UNITED STATES

Type Slide	Major Areas	Number of Historical Slides	Est. Prop. Damage (million $ adjusted to 1978 values)	Recorded Deaths
Rockslide & rockfall	White, Blue Ridge, Great Smoky, Rocky Mtns., & Appalachian Plateau	Several hundred	48	42
Rockslump & rockfall	Widespread in Central & West U.S.; prevalent in Colo. Plateau, Wyo., Mont., Southern Calif., Oreg., & Wash.	Several thousand	522	188
	Appalachian Plateau	Several thousand	562 (mainly in highway & railroad damage)	20
	Calif. Coast Ranges, Northern Rockies	Several hundred	48	—
Slump	Maine, Conn. Riv. Valley, Hudson Valley, Chicago, Red Riv., Puget Sound, Mont. glac. lakes, Alaska	About 70	225	103
	Long Island, Md., Va., Ala., S. Dak., Wyo., Mont., Colo.	Several hundred	48 (mainly to highways & foundations)	—
	Mississippi & Missouri Valleys, eastern Washington & southern Idaho	Several hundred	3	—
	Appalachian Piedmont	About 100	1	—
Debris flow & mudflow	White, Adirondack, & Appalachian Mountains	Several hundred	161	89

U.S. Geological Survey.

61

Winter storm rescue. *Courtesy United Press International.*

9. WINTER STORMS

In September, the sun leaves the Northern Hemisphere. Until the sun's return in March, polar air rules the northern continental atmosphere. Winter is here, a season broken by intervals of fine weather, and by the seasonal parade of winter storms—paralyzers of cities, destroyers of property, takers of life.

These storms are generated, as are many summer thunderstorms, along the boundaries, called "fronts," between polar and tropical air masses. The disturbances may become intense low-pressure systems, churning over tens of thousands of square miles in a great counter-clockwise sweep.

In the Pacific, these winter storms form off the east coast of Asia and travel northeastward toward Alaska. But some, particularly those forming along the mid-Pacific polar front, take a more southerly track, striking the United States as far south as Southern California. Few Pacific disturbances cross the Rockies, but some do, redeveloping to the east. One region of such redevelopment lies east of the Colorado Rockies; the storms which come out of that region are called "Colorado cyclones." Another region of storm redevelopment is east of the Canadian Rockies, from which come the so-called "Alberta cyclones." Both types take eastward paths that usually converge over the Great Lakes. The Lakes themselves are generators of severe local winter storms, and others develop from northward-drifting disturbances originating over the Gulf of Mexico and the southern plains of the U.S.

On the East Coast, winter storms often form near the coast of Virginia and the Carolinas and in the general area east of the southern Appalachians. These are the notorious Cape Hatteras storms, "nor'easters," which develop to great intensity as they move up the coast. From there they drift seaward toward Iceland, where they finally dissipate.

For some parts of the United States—the northern Rockies, for example—storms with snow followed by cold are a threat from mid-September to mid-May. During one of the colder months from November to March, it is not unusual for eight separate storms to affect some areas across the continent. Intense winter storms are frequently accompanied by cold waves, ice or glaze, heavy snow, blizzards, or a combination of these. Their common feature is the ability to completely immobilize large areas and to isolate and kill people and livestock in their path. In our northland, the severity of these storms makes them a seasonal threat. Farther south, the occasional penetration of severe winter storms into more moderate climates causes severe hardship and great loss of warm weather crops.

A Consistent Threat to Life

Nearly everyone east of the Pacific coastal ranges remembers significant winter storms—days of heavy snow, interminable blizzards, inconvenience, economic loss, and, sometimes, personal tragedy. Winter brings them all. For Wyoming, Kansas, and Texas, the blizzard of 1888 was one of the worst on record. January 11–13 in that year brought the most disastrous blizzard ever known in Montana, the Dakotas, and Minnesota, combining gale winds, blowing snow, and extreme cold into a lethal, destructive push from the Rockies eastward. Eighty people died in Iowa; Kansas lost 80 percent of its cattle. The eastern seaboard got its big storm the same year. March 11–14, 1888, saw the seaboard from Chesapeake Bay to Maine stricken with a blizzard that dumped an average of 40 inches of snow over southeastern New York and southern New England. The storm killed 200 in New York City alone; total deaths were more than 400.

But probably every winter is a bad year for some portion of the country—and winter storms can kill without breaking weather records. The danger is persistent, year after year. Of reported deaths from winter storms, more than a third are attributed to automobile and other accidents; just under one-third to overexertion, exhaustion, and consequent fatal heart attack; fewer than one-quarter to exposure and fatal freezing; and the remainder to such causes as home fires, carbon monoxide poisoning in stalled cars, falls on slippery walks, electrocution from downed wires, and building collapse. The greatest number of snow-related deaths in recent years—354—occurred in 1960; 1958 is second with 345 deaths. About half of those reported occurred in New England, New York, and Pennsylvania.

Types of Winter Storms

Ice

Freezing rain or drizzle is called an *ice storm*. Moisture falls in liquid form but freezes upon impact. The term *heavy* is used to describe an ice coating heavy enough to damage trees, overhead wires, and similar objects.

Ice storms are sometimes incorrectly referred to as "sleet storms." *Sleet* is easily identified as frozen rain drops (ice pellets) which bounce when hitting the ground or other objects. Sleet does not stick to trees and wires, but sleet in sufficient depth does cause hazardous driving conditions.

Snow

"Snow" in a forecast, without a qualifying word such as "occasional" or "intermittent," means that the fall of snow is of a steady nature and will probably continue for several hours without letup.

Snow flurries are defined as snow falling for short durations at intermittent periods; however, snowfall during flurries may reduce visibility to an eighth of a mile or less. Accumulations from snow flurries are generally small.

Snow squalls are brief, intense falls of snow and are comparable to summer rain showers. They are accompanied by gusty surface winds.

Blowing and drifting snow generally occur together and result from strong winds and falling snow or loose snow on the ground. *Blowing snow* is snow lifted from the surface by the wind and blown about so that visibility is greatly restricted.

Drifting snow is used in forecasts to indicate that strong winds will blow falling snow or loose snow on the ground into significant drifts.

Blizzards are the most dramatic and perilous of all winter storms, characterized by low temperatures and strong winds bearing large amounts of snow. Most snow accompanying a blizzard occurs as fine, powdery particles that are whipped in great quantities—sometimes reducing visibility to only a few yards.

The Wind-Chill Factor

Arctic explorers and military experts have developed the concept of the "wind-chill factor," which indicates the cooling effect of the wind. Strong winds combined with low temperatures cool exposed surfaces very rapidly. A very strong wind combined with a temperature slightly below freezing can have the same chilling effect as a temperature nearly 50°F lower in a calm atmosphere. Figure 00 illustrates the wind-chill factor for various temperatures and wind velocities. In certain areas, the National Weather Service issues this information as the "wind-chill index."

In significant wind-chill conditions, unprotected portions of the body, such as the face and hands, can chill rapidly and should be protected from the wind.

TABLE 9-1. WIND-CHILL FACTOR

Estimated Wind Speed (in mph)	Actual Thermometer Reading (°F.)											
	50	40	30	20	10	0	−10	−20	−30	−40	−50	−60
	Equivalent Temperature (°F.)											
calm	50	40	30	20	10	0	−10	−20	−30	−40	−50	−60
5	40	37	27	16	6	−5	−15	−26	−36	−47	−57	−68
10	40	28	16	4	−9	−24	−33	−46	−58	−70	−83	−95
15	36	22	9	−5	−18	−32	−45	−58	−72	−85	−99	−112
20	32	18	4	−10	−25	−39	−53	−67	−82	−96	−110	−124
25	30	16	0	−15	−29	−44	−59	−74	−88	−104	−118	−133
30	25	13	−2	−18	−33	−48	−63	−79	−94	−109	−125	−140
35	27	11	−4	−20	−35	−51	−67	−82	−98	−113	−129	−145
40	26	10	−6	−21	−37	−53	−69	−85	−100	−116	−132	−148

(Wind speeds greater than 40 mph have little additional effect.)	Little Danger (for properly clothed person.) Maximum danger of false sense of security.	Increasing Danger (Flesh may freeze within 1 minute.)	Great Danger (Flesh may freeze within 30 seconds.)

Trenchfoot and immersion food may occur at any point on this chart.

Suggested Procedures

The National Weather Service is responsible for the timely issuance of weather warnings to the public, including the approach of winter storms.

Hazardous driving (travelers') warnings are issued to indicate that falling, blowing, or drifting snow, freezing rain or drizzle, sleet or strong winds will make driving difficult.

Stockmen's warnings alert ranchers and farmers that livestock will require protection from a large accumulation of snow or ice, a rapid drop in temperature, or strong wind.

Cold wave warnings indicate an expected rapid fall in temperature within a 24-hour period which will require substantially increased protection to agricultural, industrial, commercial, and social activities. Temperature drops and minimum temperatures required to justify cold wave warnings vary with the seasons and with geographic location. Regardless of the month or the section of the country, however, a cold wave warning is a red-flag alert to the public that a forthcoming change to very cold weather will require greater than normal protective measures.

Heavy snow warnings are issued to the public when a snowfall of four inches or more is expected in a 12-hour period, or a fall of six inches or more expected in a 24-hour period. Some variations on these rules may be used in different parts of the country. Where four-inch snowfalls are common, the emphasis on heavy snow is generally associated with six or more inches of snow. In other parts of the country, where heavy snow is infrequent, or in metropolitan areas with heavy traffic, a snowfall of two or three inches will justify a heavy snow warning.

Blizzard warnings are issued when winds of at least 35 miles an hour, accompanied by considerable falling or blowing snow and temperatures of 20°F or lower, are expected to prevail for an extended time.

Severe blizzard warnings are issued when blizzards of extreme proportions are expected—winds of at least 45 miles an hour plus a great density of falling or blowing snow and temperatures of 10°F or lower.

Before a Winter Storm Occurs

Keep ahead of winter storms by listening for the latest National Weather Service bulletin on radio and television. You can do several things to prepare for storms before they happen:

- Be sure that your house will give you adequate protection from winter blasts. Before the winter season, check the insulation in ceilings and walls; install additional insulating material if necessary. Also install storm doors and windows or other weatherproofing.
- Check battery-powered equipment before a storm arrives. A portable radio or television set may be your only contact with the world outside the winter storm. Also check emergency cooking facilities and flashlights.
- Check your supply of heating fuel. Fuel carriers may not be able to move if a winter storm buries your area in snow.
- Check your food; stock an extra supply. Your supplies should include food that requires no cooking or refrigeration. There may be a power failure.
- Rural residents should make necessary trips for supplies *before* storms develop or not at all. Arrange for emergency heating in case of power failure. Be sure camp stoves and lanterns are filled.
- Dress to fit the season. If you spend much time outdoors; wear loose-fitting, lightweight, warm clothing in several layers; layers can be removed to prevent perspiring and subsequent chill. Outer garments should be water repellent and hooded. The hood should protect much of your face and cover your mouth to ensure warm breathing and protect your lungs from extremely cold air. Remember that entrapped, insulating air, warmed by body heat, is the best protection against cold. Several layers of lightweight clothing are more effective and efficient than one or two layers of thick clothing; and mittens, snug at the wrists, afford better protection than fingered gloves.
- Your automobile can be your best friend—or worst enemy— during winter storms, depending on your preparations. Get your car "winterized" before the storm season begins. Take care of all the following before winter storms strike your area:

Ignition system	Brakes
Battery	Wiper blades
Lights	Defroster
Cooling system	Snow tires (installed)
Fuel system	Chains
Lubrication	Antifreeze
Tight exhaust system	Winter-grade oil
Heater	

- Be equipped for the worst. Carry a winter storm car kit, especially if cross-country travel is anticipated or if you live in the northern states. The kit should contain at least the following:

Blankets or sleeping bags	Shovel and sack of sand
Matches and candles	Flashlight or signal light
A large, empty can with	Windshield scraper
plastic cover	Booster cables
Extra clothing	Two tow chains
High-calorie, non-	Fire extinguisher
perishable food	Catalytic heater
Compass and road maps	Facial tissue and paper
Knife and axe	towels
First-aid kit	

During a Severe Storm

- Be extremely careful to prevent overheating of coal- or oil-burning stoves, fireplaces, heaters, or furnaces. A fire in your home is very serious at any time—but doubly so during a severe winter storm. You could be left without shelter in frigid conditions.
- Stay indoors during storms and cold snaps unless you are in peak physical condition. If you must go out, avoid overexertion.
- Don't kill yourself shoveling snow. It is extremely hard work for anyone in less than prime physical condition and can bring on a heart attack, a major cause of death during and after winter storms.

If You Must Travel by Auto

Winter travel by automobile is serious business. Keep these points in mind, especially for severe storms:

- If the storm exceeds or even tests your limitations, seek refuge immediately.
- Plan your travel and select primary and alternate routes.
- Check the latest weather information on your radio.
- Try to travel with passengers, not alone.
- Travel in convoy with another vehicle, if possible.
- Always fill your gas tank before entering open country, even for a short distance.
- Drive carefully, defensively.

If a Blizzard Traps You While You Are Driving

- Don't panic.

- Stay in your vehicle. Do not attempt to walk out of a blizzard. Disorientation comes quickly in blowing and drifting snow. Being lost in open country during a blizzard is almost certain death. You are more likely to be found, and more likely to be sheltered, in your car.
- Avoid overexertion and exposure. Exertion from attempting to push your car, shovel heavy drifts, and perform other difficult chores during the strong winds, blinding snow, and bitter cold of a blizzard may cause a heart attack—even for persons in apparently good physical condition.
- Keep fresh air in your car. Freezing, wet snow and wind-driven snow can completely seal the passenger compartment, causing suffocation.
- Beware the gentle killers: carbon monoxide and oxygen starvation. Run the motor and heater sparingly, and only with the downwind window open for ventilation. During the blizzard and gales that swept Minnesota and South Dakota in March 1941, the death toll was 151. Most of these fatalities resulted from exposure and carbon monoxide poisoning in stalled cars.
- Keep watch. Do not permit all occupants of the car to sleep at one time.
- Exercise by clasping hands and moving arms and legs vigorously from time to time, and do not stay in one position for long.
- Turn on your car's dome light at night, to make the vehicle visible to work crews.

Care of Livestock

Blizzards take a frightful toll in livestock. One terrible storm that hit the Midwest in 1966 killed more than 100,000 cattle. For both humane and economic reasons, stockmen should take necessary precautions in advance of severe winter storms, including the following measures:

- Move livestock, especially young livestock, into sheltered areas. Shelter belts, properly oriented and laid out, provide better protection for range cattle than shed-type shelters, which may cause cattle to overcrowd, with consequent overheating and respiratory disorders.
- Haul extra feed to feeding areas before the storm arrives. Storm duration is the largest determinant of livestock losses; if the storm lasts more than 48 hours, emergency feed methods are

required. Range cattle are hardy and can survive extreme winter weather, provided that they have some nonconfining type of shelter from the wind and are able to feed at frequent intervals.

- Make sure stock animals can get adequate water. Autopsies of cattle killed by winter storms have shown the cause of death to be dehydration, not cold or suffocation. Because cattle cannot lick enough snow to satisfy their thirst, stockmen are advised to use heaters in water tanks.

Avalanche aftermath. *Courtesy Wide World Photos.*

10. AVALANCHES

Historically, the greatest threat of snow avalanches has been in the Alps of Europe and the Andes Mountains of South America. In Huascarán, Peru, for example, a tremendous avalanche in January 1962 thundered 13,000 vertical feet into a valley flanking an extinct volcano, devastating nine villages and killing 4,000 people and 10,000 animals.

However, avalanches are steadily becoming more of a hazard to reckon with in the United States, as logging and mining operations, resorts, and recreational homesites move into mountain areas and as Americans spend more time in skiing, snowshoeing, snowmobiling, and other winter activities. Every year, more people are caught by avalanches. Tragic accidents have struck snowmobilers, utility servicemen, hunters, and dam construction workers. Families have been buried while hiking. Two children were even buried fatally while playing in a ravine in the middle of a major eastern city.

The Avalanche Hazard

Avalanche accidents in North America fall into the following categories.

Back-Country Accidents

At present, back-country accidents account for the largest number of fatalities in North America. The victims are usually ski tourers, helicopter skiers, or mountaineers. Almost all the victims triggered their own avalanche while crossing the starting zone. In rare cases the avalanche was triggered naturally and swept into the touring party lower down in the track or runout zone. In a few instances, an avalanche overran a camp area and buried victims in their tents.

Back-country accidents can be traced to a combination of inexperience and taking calculated risks (and losing). Rescue depends on the actions of unburied survivors. Organized rescue from afar usually turns into a body-recovery operation rather than a live rescue.

Ski-Area Accidents

The victims of ski-area accidents include ski patrollers as well as the general public. Ski-patrol accidents usually result from carelessness or errors. Typically, the patroller should have used explosives to trigger a potential avalanche but decided to ski the slope instead. Sometimes the explosive test was negative, but the avalanche released during skiing.

Accidents involving the general public usually occur on uncompacted slopes. Several accidents have been caused by skiers who willingly or unknowingly skied into restricted areas. Rescue depends on fast and efficient mobilization of organized probe teams. Skiers who carry emergency electronic transmitters can be more readily rescued.

Highway Accidents

The largest number of highway-accident fatalities is suffered by highway maintenance crews. Several fatalities have resulted when the victim was plowing out debris from one avalanche and the avalanche path ran a second time. Some avalanches have enough force to toss around the largest highway-maintenance machines. The operator usually has a better chance to survive if he remains in the vehicle, although snow can be expected to crash through windows and pack tightly around the victim.

Buildings Hit by Avalanches

Mining camps have been the traditional targets of avalanches. In February of 1906, for example, separate avalanches buried the inhabitants of Wallace, Idaho, and wiped out the entire town of Mace, Colorado, killing a total of 135 people. In recent years, however, primary vulnerability has shifted to the increasing number of lodges and condominiums being constructed in avalanche paths.

Rescue in demolished buildings is very tedious and time consuming, because the snow and the building debris pack together in an almost inseparable mass. However, building debris may provide breathing space that prolongs the victim's chances of survival. In one instance, the avalanche started a fire and the victims burned to death while trapped in the debris.

Railroad Accidents

The largest single railroad avalanche disaster in North America occurred in 1910 near Wellington, Washington. This example illustrates the enormous forces of avalanches. The avalanche was not unusually large; nevertheless, two railroad cars and several locomotives were swept off their tracks. In all, 96 people perished; there were 22 survivors.

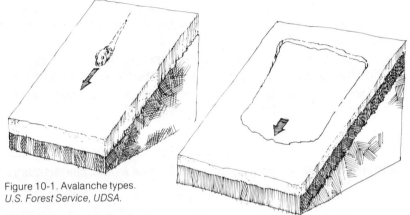

Figure 10-1. Avalanche types.
U.S. Forest Service, UDSA.

Types of Avalanche

There are two principal types of snow avalanche: loose-snow and slab. *Loose-snow* avalanches start at a point or over a small area. They grow in size, and the quantity of snow involved increases as they descend. Loose snow moves as a formless mass with little internal cohesion.

Slab avalanches, on the other hand, start when a large area of snow begins to slide at once. There is a well-defined fracture line where the moving snow breaks away from the stable snow. Slab avalanches are characterized by the tendency of snow crystals to stick together. There may be angular blocks or chunks of snow in the slide.

Practically all accidents are caused by slab avalanches. Many times the victims have triggered the avalanche themselves. Their weight on the stressed snow slab is enough to break the fragile bonds that hold it to the slope.

Terrain Factors

Four terrain factors affect snow avalanches: slope steepness, slope profile, slope aspect, and ground cover.

- Slope profile. Dangerous slab avalanches are more likely to occur on convex slopes, but may also occur on concave slopes. Short slopes may be as dangerous as long slopes.
- Slope aspect. Snow on north-facing slopes is more likely to slide in midwinter. South-facing slopes are dangerous in the spring and on sunny days. Leeward slopes are dangerous because wind-deposited snows add depth and create hard, hollow-sounding wind slabs on the slopes and overhanging cornices on the high ridges. Windward slopes generally have less snow; the snow is compacted, but usually strong enough to resist movement.
- Ground cover. Large rocks, trees, and heavy brush help anchor the snow, but avalanches can start even among trees. Slopes that were smooth and grassy in warmer weather are more dangerous when covered with snow.

TABLE 10-1. VEGETATION AS A ROUGH INDICATOR OF AVALANCHE FREQUENCY

Frequency: at least one avalanche in an interval of—	Vegetation clues
1–2 years	Bare patches, willows and shrubs, no trees higher than about 1 to 2 m. Broken timber.
2–10 years	Few trees higher than 1 to 2 m. Immature trees of disaster or pioneer species. Broken timber.
10–25 years	Predominantly pioneer species, young trees of the local climax species (increment core data).
25–100 years	Mature trees of pioneer species, young trees of the local climax species (increment core data).
Over 100 years	Increment core data.

U.S. Forest Service, USDA.

Weather Factors

Many weather factors affect the probability that a snow avalanche will occur: temperature, wind, storms, rate of snowfall, and types of snow crystal.

- Temperature. Snow persists in an unstable condition in cold temperatures. It will settle and stabilize rapidly when temperatures are near, or just above, freezing.

   Storms starting with low temperatures and dry snow, followed by rising temperatures, are more likely to cause avalanches. The dry snow at the start forms a poor bond with the slope and has insufficient strength to support heavier snow deposited later in the storm.
- Wind. Sustained winds of 15 miles per hour and higher rapidly increase the danger of avalanche. Snow plumes from ridges and peaks indicate that snow is being moved onto leeward slopes. This can create dangerous conditions.
- Storms. About 80 percent of all avalanches occur during, and shortly after, storms. Loose, dry snow slides easily. Moist, dense snow tends to settle rapidly, but during windy periods it can be dangerous.
- Rate of snowfall. Snow falling at the rate of one inch per hour or more rapidly increases avalanche danger.
- Crystal types. Snow crystals may be observed by letting them fall on a dark ski mitt or parka sleeve. Small crystals—needles and pellets—create more dangerous conditions than the usual, star-shaped crystals.

A Threat to Life

Although avalanches kill people in many ways, the great majority of fatalities are caused by suffocation. In a typical avalanche burial, little air is trapped in the space around the victim, and it is only a matter of time until he loses consciousness and dies. The weight of snow bears down on the victim's throat and chest and further accelerates respiratory failure. The snow usually packs so tightly that the victim is immobilized and must helplessly await his fate.

Some victims are killed outright or severely injured by the moving avalanche. The victim may be dashed into a tree or building or hit by flying debris. Head injuries, abdominal injuries, and broken necks, backs, and legs are common. There are also reports of

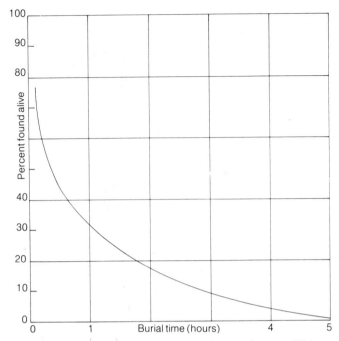

Figure 10-2. Avalanche burial time and likelihood for survival. *U.S. Forest Service, USDA.*

lung injuries caused by avalanche pressure forces. Some victims die of hypothermia, exhaustion, or shock. Fewer than 20 percent of those who are buried with no trace showing above the snow are recovered alive.

Statistics compiled in Switzerland and in the United States show that the victim's chance of survival diminishes rapidly with burial time (see Figure 10-2) and depth of burial. Statistically, after half an hour of burial, the victim's chance of surviving is about 50 percent. A victim often cannot survive a 15 minute burial in an unfavorable position (snow packed tightly around mouth and nose). This is understandable, since a person loses consciousness about 45 to 120 seconds after breathing stops. The first permanent brain damage occurs in about 4 minutes, and after 8 minutes survival is unlikely even if it is possible to restore breathing and circulation. On the other hand, if the victim is buried in a favorable position, without snow packed tightly around his mouth and nose, he may survive for hours.

Suggested Procedures

Understanding the basic types of avalanches and the contributing terrain and weather factors, as well as carefully selecting a safe route, can help you avoid being caught in a snow avalanche. It may also help you survive if you *are* caught.

Before You Go into the Mountains

It is always wise to check local weather forecasts before going to mountain recreation areas or into the back-country. To find out about current avalanche danger, contact the Forest Service snow ranger or the nearest winter sports area ski patrol.

When you enter avalanche country, be alert to the following conditions:

- Recent avalanche activity. If you see new avalanches, suspect dangerous conditions. Beware when snowballs or "cartwheels" roll down the slopes.
- Old slide paths. Generally, if an avalanche occurs once in a given area, it will occur there again. Watch for avalanche paths. Look for pushed-over small trees and trees with limbs broken off. Avoid steep, open gullies and slopes.
- Sounds and cracks. If the snow sounds hollow, particularly on a leeward slope, conditions are probably dangerous. If the snow cracks and the cracks continue to form, slab avalanche danger is high.
- New snow. Be alert to dangerous conditions when one foot or more of new snow falls.
- Old snow. When the old snow depth is sufficient to cover natural anchors such as rocks and brush, additional snow layers will slide more readily. The nature of the old snow surface is important. Rough surfaces favor stability; smooth surfaces, such as sun crusts, are less stable. A loose, underlying snow layer is more dangerous than a compacted one. Check the underlying snow layer with a ski pole, ski, or rod.
- Wet snow. Rainstorms or spring weather with warm winds and cloudy nights can warm the snow cover. The resulting free and percolating water may cause wet snow avalanches. Wet snow avalanches are more likely on south slopes and on slopes beneath exposed rock.

While You Are in the Back-Country

- Be alert to weather changes. Rapid changes in weather conditions (wind, temperature, snowfall) cause snowpack adjustments. Such adjustments may affect snowpack stability and cause an avalanche.

- The safest routes are on ridgetops and slightly on the windward side, away from cornices. Windward slopes are usually safer than leeward slopes. If travel is impossible on ridges, the next safest route is out in the valley, far from the bottom of slopes. Avoid disturbing cornices from below or above.
- If you must cross a dangerous slope, stay high and near the top. If you see avalanche fracture lines in the snow, avoid them and similar snow areas. If ascending or descending a dangerous slope, go straight up or down; do not make traverse cuts in the snow back and forth across the slope.
- Take advantage of areas of dense timber, ridges, or rocky outcrops as islands of safety. Use them for lunch and rest stops. Spend as little time as possible on open slopes.
- Snowmobiles should not cross the lower part of slopes. Do not drive a snowmobile across especially long open slopes or known avalanche paths.
- Obey signs closing slopes due to avalanche danger. Only one person at a time should cross a dangerous slope. All others should watch him. Remove ski pole straps, loosen all equipment, put on mitts and cap, and fasten clothing before you travel in any areas where there is avalanche danger. Carry and use an avalanche cord and a sectional probe.

If You Are Caught in an Avalanche

- Discard all equipment. Throw ski poles and other gear as far from you as possible.
- If you are on a snowmobile, jump clear of it.
- Make swimming motions. Try to stay on top; work your way to the side of the avalanche.
- Before coming to a stop, get your hands in front of your face and try to make an air space in the snow.
- Try to remain calm.

If You Are the Survivor

- Mark the place where you last saw victims.
- Search for victims directly downslope from where they were last seen. If they are not on the surface, scuff or probe the surface with a pole or stick.
- You are the victims' best hope for survival. Do not desert them and go for help unless help is a very short distance away. Remember, you must consider not only the time required for you

80

to get help, but also the time required for help to return. After 30 minutes, the buried victim has no more than a 50 percent chance of surviving.

If There Is More Than One Survivor

- Send one for help while the others search for the victim. Have the one who goes for help mark the route so a rescue party can follow back.
- Contact the ski patrol, local sheriff, or Forest Service.
- Administer first aid.
- Treat for suffocation and shock.

Lightning. *National Oceanic and Atmospheric Administration.*

11. LIGHTNING

Man has long marveled at lightning. References to lightning flashes are found in the literature from ancient to modern times. Yet most people are unaware of its effects on life and property.

Lightning is responsible for more deaths than any other feature of stormy weather. The general lack of respect for lightning may be attributed to the fact that limited publicity is given to deaths by lightning and that most reported incidents involve only one or two persons. Floods and tornadoes are more likely to make headlines because they affect larger areas and often cause multiple deaths, injuries, and widespread damage. Nevertheless, the average annual death toll for lightning is greater than for tornadoes or hurricanes.

Between January 1940 and December 1976, lightning is reported to have killed more than 7,500 Americans and injured more than 20,000 others. This means annual averages of about 200 killed and 550 injured. But because incomplete reporting has produced conservative numbers, the actual death toll is probably double the reported number.

One interesting fact is that 80 percent or more of both deaths and injuries from lightning occur to males. This is undoubtedly because the situations in which large groups are most often struck are quite frequently male oriented: football and baseball games, fairs, golf matches, camping, picnicking, outdoor work, and outdoor military training.

Proximity to water appears to be an important factor. Farmers, ranchers, and others in outdoor occupational groups are especially vulnerable to lightning strikes. Furthermore, use of the telephone and of CB and other radio equipment is related to lightning incidents.

Annual numbers of reported lightning deaths have been decreasing since the 1940s, and for this no adequate explanation has been found. Though the farm population has decreased, overall population and the number of people engaged in outdoor recreation such as golfing and camping have increased.

Property loss—fire and other damage to structures, aircraft damage, livestock deaths and injuries, forest fires, and other effects—is estimated at more than $100 million annually.

Lightning: A Regional Threat

The risk of being struck by lightning is greater than we tend to think. It is estimated that some 1,800 thunderstorms are in progress over the earth's surface at any given moment, and that lightning strikes the earth 100 times each second.

Some portions of the country are far more vulnerable to lightning than others. The nation's major waterways seem especially susceptible. The Mississippi, Ohio, and Hudson rivers and their drainage basins are high-risk lightning areas. So are the Colorado Rockies and the Gulf Coast—particularly around Tampa, Florida. Florida as a whole has an average of 10 or more reported lightning deaths annually. Washington, Oregon, Alaska, and Hawaii, however, seldom report lightning fatalities.

Eight states report more than one annual death per million people. Two of these—Wyoming and New Mexico—are in the West, while the remaining six are southern states: Arkansas, Florida, Louisiana, Mississippi, North Carolina, and Oklahoma. No explanation can be offered as to why South Carolina and Alabama have low numbers of lightning deaths, while adjacent states report many more.

How Lightning Works

Lightning is an effect of electrification within a thunderstorm. Basically, here's how it works:

As a thunderstorm develops, a large positive electrical charge usually concentrates in the frozen upper layers of the cloud, and a large negative charge along with a smaller positive area in the lower layers.

Normally the negative charge in the earth is greater than the negative charge in the atmosphere. However, as the thunderstorm passes over the ground, the negative charge in the base of the cloud induces a positive charge on the ground below and for several miles around the storm. (In other words, a very high voltage develops between the earth and the thundercloud.) The ground charge follows the storm around like an electrical shadow, growing stronger as the negative cloud charge increases.

The strong attraction between positive and negative charges makes the positively charged particles in the ground move up *buildings, trees, and other elevated objects* in an effort to establish a flow of current. But air, which is a poor conductor of electricity, acts as an insulator between the cloud and ground charges, preventing a flow of current until very large electrical charges are built up. Lightning occurs when the difference between the positive and negative charges—the voltage—overcomes the resistance of the insulating air, forcing the current to flow between the two charges. The potential in these instances can be as high as 100 million volts.

Lightning strokes represent a flow of current from negative to positive and may proceed from cloud to cloud, cloud to ground, or where high structures are involved, ground to cloud.

The typical cloud-to-ground stroke we see more frequently begins when a "pilot leader," too faint to be visible, advances downward from the cloud and sets up the initial portion of the stroke path. A surge of current called a "step leader" follows the pilot, moving 100 feet or more at a time toward the ground, pausing, then repeating the sequence until the conductive path of electrified (ionized) particles is near the ground. There, discharge streamers extending from the ground or from elevated objects on the ground intercept the leader path and complete the conductive channel between ground and cloud charges. When this path is complete, a return stroke leaps upward at speeds approaching that of light, illuminating the branches of the descending leader track. Because these tracks point downward, the stroke appears to come from the cloud. The bright light of the return stroke is the result of glowing particles of air energized by the stroke.

Once the channel has been established and the return stroke has ended, "dart leaders" from the cloud initiate secondary returns, until the opposing charges are dissipated or the channel is gradually broken up by air movement. Even when luminous lightning is not visible, current may continue to flow along the ionized channel set up by the initial step leader.

Suggested Procedures

A knowledge of how lightning works—usually forming an electrical arc between thunderclouds and *elevated* objects or areas of the ground—can be very helpful to you in reducing your chances of being struck by lightning. Whenever lightning strikes, it can be dangerous. The first line of defense is to know when and where you can be hit by lightning.

Some parts of the day are riskier than others. According to studies, about 70 percent of lightning injuries and deaths occur in the afternoon, 20 percent between 6:00 P.M. and midnight, 10 percent between 7 A.M. and noon, and fewer than 1 percent from midnight to 6:00 A.M. Lightning is also far more common from May through September than in other months.

Armed with these facts, protect yourself when a thunderstorm threatens. Get inside a home or large building, or inside an all-metal (not convertible) vehicle. Inside a home, avoid using the telephone, except for emergencies. If you are outside, with no time to reach a safe building or an automobile, follow these rules:

- Do not stand underneath a natural lightning rod such as a tall, isolated tree in an open area.
- Avoid projecting above the surrounding landscape, as you would do if you were standing on a hilltop, in an open field, on the beach, or fishing from a small boat.
- Get out of and away from open water.
- Get away from tractors and other metal farm equipment.
- Get off and away from motorcycles, scooters, golf carts, and bicycles. Put down golf clubs.
- Stay away from wire fences, clotheslines, metal pipes, rails, and other metallic paths which could carry lightning to you from some distance away.
- Avoid standing in small, isolated sheds or other small structures in open areas.
- In a forest, seek shelter in a low area under a thick growth of small trees. In open areas, go to a low place such as a ravine or valley. Be alert for flash floods.
- If you're hopelessly isolated in a level field or prairie and you feel your hair stand on end—indicating lightning is about to strike—drop to your knees and bend forward putting your hands on your knees. *Do not* lie flat on the ground. This will ensure that as small an area as possible is touching the ground and will minimize the danger of your body acting as a conductor.

12. HEAT WAVES

Weather depends largely on the position of the jet stream. In winter, the jet stream shifts southward over the United States, bringing in its wake a succession of stormy low-pressure systems. However, as the continent warms with the approach of summer, the jet stream shifts northward and higher temperatures prevail: the season for heat waves has arrived.

East of the Rockies, heat waves tend to be periods of high temperature and high humidity—those oppressive, muggy days when human comfort is only an empty expression. However, the worst heat waves have been catastrophically dry.

In the Southwest, heat waves are the result of desert conditions and are characteristically dry. Sometimes these heat waves are general and persistent. California's worst heat waves are produced when a high-pressure system over the Nevada desert sends hot air southwestward through the mountain passes.

Man's Vulnerability to Heat

Most people survive heat waves, and they tend to remember them only as periods of sweltering discomfort; seldom are we impressed by death tolls resulting from heat waves. However, in a "normal" year about 175 Americans die from summer heat and too much sun—"excessive heat" is the vital statistics category. Among the natural hazards, only winter storms and lightning—not hurricanes, tornadoes, floods, or earthquakes—take a greater average toll.

And the threat is widespread in the U.S.: June 1962—five days of 100° plus in 17 eastern states killed 160; July 1–13, 1966—record temperatures in New York City left hundreds dead; July 1916—a heat wave scorched Chicago, killing 305; July 1934—a three-week heat wave in the St. Louis, Missouri, area killed 415; June 1931—a heat wave with temperatures above 100° struck 12 midwestern states, leaving 1,016 dead. And the statistics continue, nationwide. One heat wave that struck New York City some years ago took 33 lives—including some drownings caused by overcrowding at beaches.

Studies show that heat waves afflict people of all ages. However, the severity of the reaction tends to increase with age—heat cramps in a 17 year-old may be heat exhaustion in someone 40 years old, and heat stroke in a person over 60.

The body tries to adapt to varying temperatures by adjusting the amount of salt in its perspiration. In hot weather, the idea is to lose enough water to keep the body cool but to create the least possible chemical disturbance. Salt helps body tissues retain water, and if the body loses too much salt through perspiration, the person may be subject to dehydration and the further overheating that follows.

Because females typically excrete less perspiration and therefore less salt, heat syndrome usually strikes fewer of them than it does males.

For people with heart disease, climatic stress is more dangerous. In a hot, humid environment, impaired evaporation and water loss hamper thermal regulation, while physical exertion and heart failure increase the body's rate of heat production—often a lethal combination.

Suggested Procedures

Coping with a heat wave is largely a matter of taking sensible precautions beforehand and avoiding foolish risks when temperatures and humidity rise. Here are some suggestions:

Before a Heat Wave Strikes

- If you have any question about your ability to withstand heat, have a complete physical examination before the onset of hot weather.
- Heatproof your home. Have your air-conditioning system checked before summer. Install sun shades over windows, if necessary.

When It Gets Hot

- Slow down. Your body can't do its best in high temperatures and humidities—and it might do its worst.
- Avoid thermal shock. Acclimatize yourself gradually to warmer weather. Treat yourself extra gently during those critical first two or three hot days.

- Don't get too much sun. Sunburn makes the job of heat dissipation that much harder for your body.
- Dress for summer. Lightweight, light-colored clothing reflects heat and sunlight and helps your body maintain its normal temperature.
- Put less fuel on your inner fires. Foods such as proteins increase the production of body heat and the loss of water.
- Don't dry out. Heat-wave weather can wring you out before you know it. Drink plenty of water while the hot spell lasts.
- Stay salty. Unless you're on a salt-restricted diet, take an occasional salt tablet or some salt solution when you've worked up a sweat.
- Because physical stress increases with exposure time, try to get out of the heat for at least a few hours each day. If you can't do this at home, drop in on a cool store, restaurant, or theater—anything to keep your exposure time down.
- Watch children carefully. Babies and small children have more surface (skin) area per unit of body volume than adults. Therefore, they can lose body heat faster in cold weather and they can also dissipate heat faster in hot weather. On the other hand, they can also be overcome by intense heat faster than adults. It is often difficult to persuade parents that babies don't always have to be bundled up; nevertheless, it is important to keep little children cool and comfortable in extremely hot weather.

When Heat Illness Threatens

- Heed your body's early warnings that heat illness is on the way. Reduce your level of activity immediately and get to a cooler environment.
- If you begin to feel faint, weak, and breathless, cool off immediately. Take a cool bath and drink some lightly salted water. If you do not feel better soon, *get help*—before you become helpless.

Know the symptoms of heat syndrome and be able to administer first aid to others (see p. 209). You must be able to deal with heat exhaustion and heat stroke quickly, or the victim can be in real trouble. Remember: Red + Hot + Dry = Die.

Active volcano. *Courtesy Italian State Tourist Office.*

13. VOLCANOES

Volcanoes are very rare but very potent. Active volcanoes are few in number, and the areas near most are sparsely populated. Most of the largest eruptions have occurred in uninhabited areas, such as Alaska's Valley of Ten Thousand Smokes (1912) and Bezymianny, Kamchatka (1956). But, as one authority on volcanoes points out, such an eruption in a densely populated area would produce "a catastrophe of unheard-of proportions."[1]

Nevertheless, some volcanoes have been enormously destructive. Among the worst in recorded history were these:[2]

- Vesuvius, A.D. 79, which destroyed Pompeii (burying it until its rediscovery in 1595) and killed 16,000.
- Skaptar Jokull (Iceland), 1783, which killed 10,000 people and most of the island's livestock, and even destroyed crops 1,000 kilometers away in Scotland.
- Tambora (Sumbawa Island, Indonesia), 1815, by which 12,000 perished directly and up to 70,000 died later as a result of the destruction of crops and subsequent famine.
- Mt. Pelée (Martinique), 1902, whose volcanic flows completely destroyed the city of St. Pierre in a matter of minutes, killing all but two of its 30,000 inhabitants.
- La Soufriére (St. Vincent Island, British West Indies), also 1902, which took 2,000 lives and completed the extinction of the Carib Indians.
- Mt. Lamington (Papua, New Guinea), 1951: 6,000 dead.
- Mt. Agung (Bali, Indonesia), 1963, which took 1,500 lives.
- Villarica (Chile), 1963–64, which forced 30,000 to evacuate their homes.
- Taal (Philippines), 1965, which claimed 500 lives.

The Active Volcano

Volcanic activity creates a number of different phenomena. Geysers and hot springs are caused by the heating of ground water. There are also gas emissions from vents and fissures. And solid material such as scoriae (cinders), bits of lava, and ashes are ejected into the atmosphere. The flow of lava down volcano slopes often accompanies spectacular and violent eruptions.[3]

When mountains are being formed, rocks in the earth's crust are forced to great depths, where increased temperature and pressure convert them into a liquid called magma. Once formed, magma exerts pressure on the surrounding solid rock. If the rock has fissures running toward the surface of the earth, magma surges upward.[4] Rising from depths of tens to hundreds of miles, this magma is the ultimate cause of volcanoes. Deposited near the vent or vents from which it is ejected, the magma eventually forms a hill or mountain—a volcano. Such mountains are being formed all the time. In 1943 Paricutin developed in a cornfield in Mexico. In most cases, however, volcanic eruptions occur at the sites of existing volcanic cones.

There are three chief dangers posed by volcanic eruptions: lava flows, airborne clouds of volcanic debris, and pyroclastic rocks and flows.

Lava flows are the most familiar product of volcanic eruptions. They are essentially the overflow of magma from the crater of a volcano or from an associated vent. Lava flows can be nonexplosive (effusive) or explosive (eruptive). Suboceanic volcanoes are usually effusive; those on islands and continental land masses, eruptive.

The lava flow from an effusive volcano is relatively rapid near the source, where the lava is very hot, but farther from the source it cools, becoming covered with a viscous skin which slows and eventually stops the flow.[5]

Lava flows produced by an eruption are generally preceded by ejection of cinders and lava fragments, followed by a quiescent period during which collapsed material from the crater walls temporarily blocks the opening. Then, after a short interval, a violent eruption occurs, producing lava fountains as much as a half mile high. Lava flows formed in this manner are very fluid and travel very rapidly. For example, an eruption of Vesuvius in 1779 caused a river of lava 65 feet wide, which traveled at 25 to 30 feet per second.[6]

Airborne ash from volcanoes contains cinders and pyroclastic rocks. Pyroclastic rocks are formed by the rapid expansion of gas in the lava, or by the explosion of steam when lava runs into the sea. These materials are blown into the air, where they remain suspended for long periods, but eventually they fall back to earth.

Pyroclastic flows also occur when solid particles suspended in a gas behave like a liquid. The resulting fluid ash moves with great speed, even over a gentle slope.[7] Such flows deposit material very rapidly to form ignimbrite sheets, rock layers that may be as much as 1,600 feet thick. The Katmai, Alaska, eruption in 1912 produced 300 million cubic feet of ignimbrite in 60 hours. Yellowstone Park is an area of broad ignimbrite sheets. In the Lamar River area of the park there are 27 distinct forests buried, one on top of another, by successive pyroclastic deposits.

The Present Threat of Volcanoes

Figure 13-1 shows the location of the world's active volcanoes. While 79 percent of all active volcanoes are in the Pacific area, their distribution is very irregular, with about 45 percent in the islands of the western Pacific and only 17 percent along the Pacific coasts of North and South America. There are large gaps between Alaska and the Cascade Mountains, and between the Cascades and northern Chile, but these regions contain numerous extinct volcanoes. The Indonesian islands are especially rich in active volcanoes (14 percent), and Hawaii and Samoa account for 3 percent.

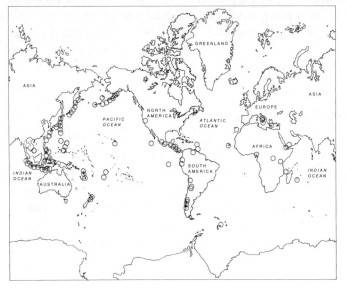

Figure 13-1. Volcanoes that have erupted since 1900.

93

The most active volcanoes in the populated areas of the United States are those in Hawaii. These include the Haleakala volcano on Maui and the Hualalai, Mauna Loa, and Kilauea volcanoes on Hawaii. Haleakala last erupted in 1750 and Haulalai around 1800, whereas Mauna Loa has erupted once every 3.6 years on the average since 1832 and Kilaeua has been in constant activity with at least 32 eruptions since 1750.

Most of the potentially dangerous volcanoes in the mainland United States lie along the crest of the Cascade Mountains of Washington, Oregon, and California. Most are inactive and do not appear to pose a threat to the surrounding countryside, but they have a long history of lava flows and are potentially dangerous. They also have a potential for producing choking clouds of fine ash over vast areas, suffocating or severely affecting the breathing of people within 10 to 20 miles. Dozens of ash layers from the Cascade Volcanoes have been recognized and mapped by members of the U.S. Geological Survey (USGS). The debris from the 6,600 year-old eruption at Crater Lake was showered more than six inches deep over much of central Oregon. Under similar conditions today, Mt. Rainier or Mt. Hood could shower a layer of debris at least six inches deep over downtown Seattle or Portland. The loss of life and property would, of course, be enormous.[9]

Of far graver danger in the Cascades is the possibility of large-scale eruptions that produce pyroclastic flows. These flows travel downslope along the ground at speeds up to 80 miles an hour and are capable of traveling tens of miles from their volcano. Crater Lake, for example, was the source of large volumes of pyroclastic flow material that traveled nearly 50 miles from the volcano.

Suggested Procedures

Populated areas surrounding the active volcanoes of Hawaii, the Pacific Northwest, and Alaska are endangered by the threat of future volcanic activity.

People and property in the immediate vicinity of a volcano could be endangered by lava flows, pyroclastic flows, debris flows, mud flows, and floods. People and property within 50 to 75 miles could be seriously affected by the fallout of airborne ash and flood-transported debris; the former could cause serious respiratory problems or even suffocation, and while both ash and debris could ruin crops and reduce productivity for several years.

94

If the fallout were sufficient, buildings would collapse and people and animals would be entrapped.

In short, all life and property is endangered by volcanic eruptions, and the extent of the devastation is chiefly dependent on the size of the eruption.

At first glance, it might seem that the best advice is to avoid going near a dormant volcano at all, and certainly to avoid building cities in areas where there is the possibility of volcanic activity. But because eruptions have been few and far between, the risks have either been ignored or have seemed worth the taking. Certainly people do live in areas of potential danger. Therefore, methods of keeping losses in life and property to a minimum are in order. The following are suggested procedures to follow if a volcanic emergency should occur:

- People must be prepared to leave as quickly as possible when volcanic activity threatens—especially those who live in valleys near the slopes of a volcanic mountain. If you hear rumbling and the ground begins to tremble, run as fast as possible for high ground and keep running. Since roads usually go directly beside rivers and along canyon floors where the threat of lava flows is greatest, use your auto to escape *only* when you are certain of a safe route, or when there is no other alternative.
- Cooperate fully with local authorities and emergency units directing evacuation and rescue operations.
- Ashfall warnings will be issued through the media. This hazard is greater for objects and buildings than for people. Close doors, windows and fireplace dampers, but do not turn on all lights: the power drain may overwhelm utilities. For normally healthy people, breathing volcanic ash in small amounts is merely unpleasant and irritating. The mouth and nose can be covered with a damp cloth or an industrial dust mask. Wear goggles to protect your eyes (a scuba mask would probably serve), and cover skin surfaces, especially in acid rains. Upon entering a shelter, remove clothing and wash exposed skin and eyes thoroughly in clear water.
- Avoid low-lying areas, where toxic gases or carbon dioxide may be collecting, and stay out of gas and steam clouds. If you are caught in a steam cloud, protect your mouth and nose as well as possible; do not breathe deeply.
- If you cannot avoid volcanic debris or rocks scattering down hillsides, roll up in a tight ball and protect your head. Scientists

in ordinary clothing have been struck by hot lava and not seriously injured when they took blows on backs or limbs.

- Survival from a lava flow may be impossible, but if you have no way to escape, try grabbing onto a large rock, tree, or anything being borne along on top of the mass. There may be a chance of riding out a flow until rescue comes.
- Do not return to a hazardous area until you have been assured by knowledgeable authority that the danger is past. Volcanoes are notorious for multiple eruptions once volcanic activity has begun.

Notes

1. Cliff Ollier, *Volcanoes* (Cambridge, Mass., and London: The MIT Press, 1969), p. 154.

2. Gordon A. MacDonald, *Catalogue of the Active Volcanoes of the World Including Solfatara Fields: Part III, Hawaiian Islands,* International Volcanological Association (Naples, Italy: Stabilimento. Tipografico Franceseo Giannini & Figli, 1956), pp. vii, 2, 7, 16–18, 26–27.

3. Ollier, *Volcanoes.* pp. 153–54.

4. A. Rittman, *Volcanoes and Their Activity,* trans. E. A. Vincent (New York: John Wiley & Sons, Inc., 1962), pp. 1–19.

5. Ibid., pp. 196–97, 209–20.

6. Ibid., p. 19.

7. Ibid., pp. 30–33.

8. Dwight R. Crandall and Howard H. Waldron, "Volcanic Hazards in the Cascade Range," *Geologic Hazards and Public Problems,* Conference Proceedings, May 27–28, 1969, Office of Emergency Preparedness, Region Seven.

9. Ollier, *Volcanoes,* pp. 73–75.

14. FIRE

Fire is a major problem worldwide. But the United States leads all major industrialized countries in per capita deaths and property loss from fire.

Many fires are spectacularly destructive and take many lives in minutes or just a few hours: a tanker ship exploded in Texas City, Texas, killing 552 and destroying $100 million worth of property in the area; a nightclub fire in Boston killed 491 and injured hundreds of others; a hotel in Atlanta was gutted, taking 119 lives and injuring 90; a terrible fire swept a hospital in Effingham, Illinois, killing 77 people, 20 of them babies in the newborn ward; 168 died in a deadly circus tent fire in Hartford, Connecticut; a fire at the Ohio State penitentiary killed 322—and the list continues. But the greatest toll is taken day by day in fires that take a single household, business, or apartment building.

During each hour more than 300 destructive fires will occur somewhere in the United States; one person will have died and 34 will be injured, some crippled or disfigured for life. Annually 12,000 lives are claimed by fire in the United States.

Ignorance and indifference contribute to the fire problem in the United States: more than half the nation's fires are caused by carelessness. For example, few private homes have fire extinguishers, and even fewer have fire-detection systems. Furthermore, when fire strikes, ignorance of what to do often increases the hazards.

Early Warning: A Key to Safe Escape

Over and over it has been shown that the family warned early enough can escape a fire. If the warning is not given—if the family is asleep when fire breaks out—there probably will be a fatality. Most fire victims never see the flames; they die in their sleep, asphyxiated by combustion products and toxic gases.

The Los Angeles Fire Department studied more than 4,000 home fires and found that three out of every four smoldered for minutes or hours, sometimes never breaking out in flames. The smoke and toxic gases build up, spread throughout the home, and block escape from the bedrooms. Often, when flames do break out and an alarm is given, it's too late. The family is trapped.

But this does not have to happen, now that relatively inexpensive home fire alarm systems are available.

Smoke detectors must form the backbone of the home fire-alarm system. The smoke detector senses an abnormal amount of smoke or invisible combustion gases. Only the smoke detector can warn of both smoldering and flaming fires while there is still time to get out. Heat detectors are also available, but because they sense the temperature of the fire only after it has already reached the flaming stage, they will not give early enough warning. They may be cheaper, but they will not give the protection you need. However, heat detectors can be useful as *supplements* to smoke detectors, and may be installed in attic spaces, garages, and other areas where fires will not immediately block safe escapes. Smoke detectors, although important in all homes, are essential in mobile homes, small apartments, and small houses, which quickly fill with lethal smoke from even a small fire.

There are now many types of these smoke detectors on the market, and you can buy them from any number of nearby sources. Many of them are very good, very reliable, and inexpensive. The important thing is that they be smoke detectors,

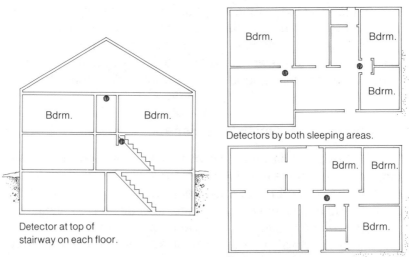

Detector at top of
stairway on each floor.

Detectors by both sleeping areas.

Single detector by bedrooms.

Figure 14-1. Smoke detectors: recommended locations. *National Fire Prevention and Control Administration.*

tested and labeled by the Underwriters' Laboratories (UL) or Factory Mutual (FM). Only the smoke detector can sound an alarm early enough to give you a chance to escape. The UL or FM label is evidence that the device has been tested for sensitivity and reliability. (Figure 14-1 shows recommended locations for their installation.)

Suggested Procedures

Each year, with the onset of cold weather and the increased use of heating equipment comes an increase in destructive fires. Peak mortality rates usually occur in January; the lowest death tolls are recorded in July or August. Regardless of the time of year, however, the following measures will help protect your family.

Household Fire Safety

All fires require three ingredients: fuel, heat, and oxygen. Therefore, you can best prevent fire in your home or apartment by preventing these elements from coming together. Consider the following procedures to keep your home safe from fire:

- To prevent the danger of spontaneous ignition, dispose of rags even slightly saturated with oil, polishes, or other flammable liquids. Put them in outdoor garbage cans to be carried away soon.
- Keep wastebaskets emptied. Remove all trash and stored items that have outlived their usefulness, particularly from around furnaces and heaters and from hallways and exit areas.
- Do not store gasoline or flammable cleaners in glass containers. They can break. Do not keep more flammable liquids on hand than you really need.
- Never use a combustible liquid to "freshen" any fire or to start a fire in a stove not designed for liquid fuel.
- Have your heating equipment serviced each year before cold weather sets in, or at the first sign of trouble. Have chimneys and pipes checked, and be sure that furnace parts are oiled, cleaned, and adjusted as required.
- Exercise care in the use of electricity. Do not overload electrical circuits with many appliances; use only appropriate fuses, and do not hang electrical cords over nails or run them under carpets. Have a competent electrician replace cords that have begun to fray or crack.

- Exercise extreme care with smoking materials and matches. These are major causes of destructive fire. Do not leave them where children can reach them.
- Invest in fire extinguishers, escape ladders, and—most important—early-warning fire detectors and alarm devices. Check them regularly: put new batteries in battery-operated smoke detectors, and have fire extinguishers recharged according to instructions.
- Make sure all windows and doors needed for emergency escape can be opened easily from the inside.
- Check your home for fire safety before you go to bed.

Planning for Every Family Member

No house can be made completely fireproof, and not everyone instinctively flees from a burning home. Children often panic and hide in closets or under beds. All families should therefore have some sort of family fire-escape plan.

The time to plan for a fire emergency is before it happens, when everyone is calm and rational. That's when escape routes can be planned and a safe evacuation practiced. Have a family conference soon. Planning won't help after a fire. Your conference doesn't have to be long or complicated; just emphasize the most important fact: *Lives come first.* Here are some points to include in your planning:

- Emphasize that everyone must get out immediately—even if they only *suspect* that there's a fire. Making certain that everybody is safe is the first consideration. Even calling the fire department should wait until everyone has been alerted.
- Draw a floor plan of your home or apartment building and mark an escape route *and* an alternate route from each room in the house. Explain how to escape through windows, breaking glass with a heavy object if necessary. Exiting through a second-story window may require a rope or folding ladder. Never go out a window head first. Back out of the window and hang from the sill with your hands before dropping to the ground. Dropping from a window should be a last resort. If you live in an apartment building, stress the importance of using staircases or fire escapes, *never elevators,* during a fire.
- Give special consideration to very young children and elderly people when planning escape routes. The death rate from fire among children under five years and the elderly over 65 is three

100

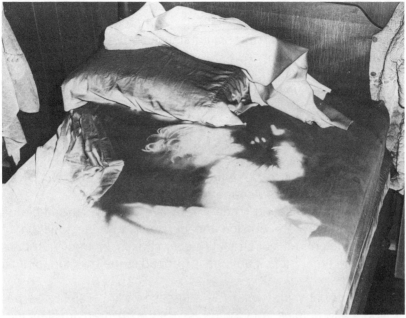
Most fire victims never see the flames. *Courtesy Willoughby, Ohio, Police Dep't.*

times that of the rest of the population. Older children should look out for younger ones. Adults who can't walk should sleep on the ground floor of a house, where it will be easy for them to get out. Only the most agile should sleep in basement or attic bedrooms.

- Everyone should sleep with bedroom doors closed. A closed door can delay the spread of fire and its deadly gases and smoke for the few precious minutes needed for escape. Also sleep with a window partially open—so that a fire cannot pull all the oxygen from the room.
- Clothing afire is a prelude to tragedy. Buy garments, such as children's sleepwear, that meet federal flammability standards. Do not wear (or permit children to wear) loose, frilly garments if there is any chance at all of accidental contact with a stove burner or other source of fire.
- Agree on a way in which any family member can sound an alarm—pounding on walls, yelling, whistling, and so on.
- Instruct family members not to waste time getting dressed or collecting prized possessions.
- Make sure that every family member knows how to test a door. If panels or knobs are warm (keep the hand on the door for at

least five seconds to determine this), keep the door closed and use an alternate escape route. If not, brace your foot and hip against the door and open it cautiously to prevent superheated air from blowing it open.

- Hold a practice drill once you have set up escape routes; then repeat drills every six months. Also practice your emergency escape plan at night, in the dark. Develop a realistic plan. For instance, make sure the children can actually open and escape from the window you expect them to use in case the normal way out is blocked. Don't expect too much of children, but at least teach them to close their bedroom doors and wait by an open window until someone can reach them.
- Decide on a meeting place where everyone will assemble as soon as they are outside the house. Know the location of nearby telephones or street fire-alarm boxes. Instruct your family to tell firefighters if anyone is trapped in the building, or if all are safe.
- Tell your babysitter what to do in case of fire. Tell him or her about alternate escape routes, where the children are sleeping, the importance of lives over property, the location of the telephone, and where you can be reached. Write down the telephone number of the fire department and tape it to the receiver of each telephone.

When Fire Strikes

When a fire does occur, your preparation will pay off. If you have adequate warning, your family will probably evacuate quickly. Nevertheless, a fire is always frightening, and the unexpected can happen. Here are some procedures to follow if you can't get away from a fire right away:

- Try to put out a fire only if you can extinguish it quickly, in the first flash (See Tables 14-1 and 14-2). If the fire gets out of control even a little, get yourself and others to safety and leave the fire to the fire department. Lives are always the first consideration. Fire extinguishers should be hung near the door through which you would escape.
- Remember that smoke is the greatest danger in a fire, because it either disables victims or blocks their escape. Not only are the gases from a fire poisonous, the stress of an emergency also makes you breathe harder, so you tend to take in more of these gases. Remember to stay near the floor, where the air will be breathable. Keep low. Act quickly. Stay calm.

TABLE 14-1. FIRE EXTINGUISHERS FOR THE HOME

Types of Extinguisher	Classes of Fire
Water Freezes in low temperature unless treated with anti-freeze solution. Usually weighs over 20 pounds and is heavier than any other extinguisher mentioned.	Fights class A fires only
Standard Dry Chemical Also called Ordinary or Regular Dry Chemical (Sodium Bicarbonate) Clean residue immediately after using the extinguisher so that sprayed material will not be affected.	Fights class B and C fires
Purple K Dry Chemical (Potassium Bicarbonate) Has greatest initial fire-stopping power of the extinguishers mentioned for class B fires. Clean residue immediately after using the extinguisher so sprayed material will not be affected.	Fights class B and C fires
Multipurpose Dry Chemical (Ammonium Phosphates) Only extinguisher which fights all three classes of fires. Clean residue immediately after using the extinguisher so sprayed material will not be affected.	Fights class A, B and C fires

Class A is fire in ordinarily combustible materials (paper, wood, cloth, and many plastics).
Class B is fire in flammable liquids, gases, and greases.
Class C is fire in electrical appliances and equipment (faulty wiring, as in a TV).

General Services Administration.

TABLE 14-2. COMMON HOUSEHOLD FIRES AND HOW TO FIGHT THEM

Type of Fire	What to Do
Food in the oven	Close the oven door. Turn off the heat.
Smoke from an electric motor or appliance	Pull the plug or otherwise turn off the electricity. If flaming, use water after the electricity is off.
Smoke from a television	Keep clear; the picture tube may burst. Call the fire department. Shut off power to the circuit.
Small pan fire on the stove	Cover with a lid or plate. Turn off the heat.
Deep fat fryer	Turn off the heat and cover with a metal lid if you can approach it. Don't attempt to move the appliance. Don't fight the fire. Evacuate, then call the fire department.

National Fire Prevention and Control Administration.

- If you are forced to remain in a room, stay near a slightly opened window. Place towels (wet, if possible) or cloths in the door cracks. To reach the other side of a smoke-filled room, crawl with your head about 18 inches above the floor. Cover your nose and mouth with a pillow or wet cloth, or hold your breath.

Figure 14-2. Escape by staying close to the floor.

- Escape through normal exits if you can; otherwise, use a window (See Figure 14-3.) Even from a second floor the window sill is usually not more than 13 feet from the ground; an average person, hanging by fingertips, will have a drop of only about 6 feet. Always lower small children as far as possible before dropping them. *Don't* go first and expect them to follow. A child may panic and go back into the room. Also, be sure to close the door before opening a window. Otherwise, smoke may be drawn into the room by the draft.

Figure 14-3. Window-escape technique.

- Call the fire department as soon as everyone is out of the house. Use an alarm box or a neighbor's phone. Speak clearly and plainly, making sure you give your full name and address.

- Watch children very carefully, being sure they don't reenter the house to rescue a pet or a toy.
- If people are trapped in a burning building before help arrives, help them *if you can do it safely*. But a rescue attempt by an untrained person through heavy smoke and flames is nearly always hopeless. Try to wait for the fire department. Equipped with special clothing and breathing apparatus, firefighters have a much better chance of reaching those who are trapped and bringing them out alive.

Fire in a High-Rise Building

These days, newer buildings more than three or four stories high are usually built of materials that will not burn or collapse even if a severe fire occurs. Normally a fire in such a "fire-resistive" building will be confined to the apartment where it started, provided

High-rise fire. *Courtesy Wide World Photos.*

the apartment door is closed. Thus, if the fire is not in your apartment, you could probably stay there in complete safety.

However, if smoke begins to fill your apartment or office, follow these procedures:

- Call the fire department immediately, giving the street address as well as the floor location. Don't assume somebody else has already called them. Use a fire extinguisher only if you still have an escape route.

- Test your door. If you feel the corridor can be used, alert other occupants on your floor and go to the closest stairway. Be sure to close your door and the stairway door behind you. *Don't* try to use the elevators.

- If you encounter smoke in your descent, use other escape routes. If these are also blocked by smoke, return to your room, closing all doors between you and the fire. Vents through which the smoke could reach you should be closed or otherwise blocked. Open a window (break one, if necessary). You must have fresh air! Wait in your room for rescue.

TABLE 14-3. TOLERANCE TO SELECTED COMBUSTION PRODUCTS

Products	Minutes	Hazardous Levels for Times Indicated		
		½ Hour	1–2 Hours	8 Hours
Heat (°F.)	284	212	150	120
Oxygen (%)	6	11	14	15
Carbon Dioxide (ppm)	50,000	40,000	35,000	32,000
Carbon Monoxide (ppm)	3,000	1,600	800	100
Sulphur Dioxide (ppm)	400	150	50	8
Nitrogen Dioxide (ppm)	240	100	50	30
Hydrogen Chloride (ppm)	1,000	1,000	40	7
Hydrogen Cyanide (ppm)	200	100	50	2

Note: There is considerable variation among investigators as to what level of a particular gas constitutes a life hazard.
Calvin H. Yuill, "Physiological Effects of Products of Combustion," American Society of Safety Engineers Journal, *February 1974. By permission.*

15. NUCLEAR ATTACK

Strife and tension abound in many parts of the world, and despite continuing efforts to achieve and maintain peace, a nuclear attack upon the United States remains a distinct possibility. The weapons of modern warfare have become increasingly powerful and numerous. Potential aggressors can deliver nuclear warheads accurately on targets up to 8,000 miles away.

The first step in preparing for a possible nuclear attack is to understand the major hazards during and after the attack.

When a nuclear bomb or missile explodes, the main effects produced are intense light (flash), heat, blast, and radiation. The strength of these effects depends on (1) the size and type of the weapon, (2) how far away the explosion is, (3) the weather conditions (sunny or rainy, windy or still), (4) the terrain (whether the ground is flat or hilly), and (5) the height of the explosion (high in the air or near the ground).

All nuclear explosions produce light, heat, blast, and gamma radiation immediately. In addition, explosions high in the air create small radioactive particles, but these particles have no real effect on humans until months or years later, if at all.

However, when a nuclear weapon explodes near the ground, great quantities of pulverized earth and other debris are sucked up into the nuclear cloud. There the radioactive gases produced by the explosion condense on and into this debris, producing radioactive fallout particles. Within a short time, these particles fall back to earth—the larger ones first, the smaller ones later. On their way down, and after they reach the ground, these radioactive particles give off invisible radiation—like X-rays—too much of which can injure people or kill them. But because these particles give off most of their radiation quickly, the first few hours or days after an attack would be the most dangerous period.

In dangerously affected areas the particles themselves would look like grains of salt or sand; but the radiation they would give off could not be seen, tasted, smelled, or felt. Special instruments would be required to detect the rays and measure their intensity.

Nuclear blast. *Courtesy Wide World Photos.*

The distribution of fallout particles after a nuclear attack would depend on wind currents, weather conditions, and other factors. There is no way of predicting which areas of the country would be affected by fallout, or how soon the particles would fall back to earth at a particular location.

Some communities might get a heavy accumulation of fallout; others—even in the same general area—might get little or none. No area in the United States could be sure of *not* getting fallout, and it is probable that some fallout particles would be deposited on most of the country.

Areas close to a nuclear explosion might receive fallout within 15 to 30 minutes. It might take 5 to 10 hours or more for the particles to drift down on a community 100 or 200 miles away.

Generally, the first 24 hours after fallout began to settle would be the most dangerous period to a community's residents. The heavier particles falling during that time would still be highly radioactive and give off strong radiation. The lighter particles falling later would have lost much of their radiation high in the atmosphere.

The Threat of Nuclear Fallout

People close to a nuclear explosion probably would be killed or seriously injured by the blast, or by the heat or initial radiation of the nuclear fireball.

People a few miles away—in the "light damage" area of the explosion—would be endangered by the blast and heat, and by fires that the explosion might start. But most would survive these hazards. Nevertheless, they would be further endangered by radioactive fallout.

Studies show that in any nuclear attack an enemy might launch against the United States, tens of millions of Americans would be outside the immediate damage areas. To them—and to people in the "light damage" areas who survived the blast, heat, and fire—radioactive fallout would be the main danger.

Therefore, the fate of people involved in a nationwide nuclear attack would depend primarily upon their nearness to a nuclear explosion.

Many studies have demonstrated that the food and water available after an attack would sustain survivors. (However, food shortages might occur in some areas, until food was shipped there from other areas.) Most of the nation's remaining food supplies would be usable after an attack. Radiation passes through food without contaminating it; therefore, the only danger would be the actual swallowing of fallout particles that happened to be on the food itself (or on the can or package containing the food), and these could be wiped or washed off.

Water systems might be affected by fallout, but the risk would be small, especially if a few simple precautions were taken. Water stored in covered containers and water in covered wells would not be contaminated, because the fallout particles could not get into the water. Even if the containers were not covered (such as buckets or bathtubs filled with emergency supplies of water) but were indoors, it is highly unlikely that fallout particles could get into them.

Practically all the particles that dropped into open reservoirs, lakes, and streams (or into open containers or wells) would settle to the bottom. Any that didn't would be removed when the water was filtered before being pumped to consumers. Some radioactive material might dissolve in the water, but this would be of concern for only a few weeks.

Milk contamination from fallout is not expected to be a serious problem. Cows might graze on contaminated pasture and swallow fallout particles that contain some radioactive elements, and as a result, their milk might be harmful. But canned and powdered milk would be generally accessible and should be used for a few weeks if authorities say that the regular milk supply is contaminated.

In summary, the danger of receiving harmful doses of fallout radiation through food, water, or milk is relatively small. Therefore, people suffering from extreme hunger or thirst should not be denied these necessities after an attack, even if the only available supplies might contain fallout particles.

The Radiation Hazard

The invisible gamma rays given off in a nuclear detonation, and the alpha and beta radiation from fallout particles can cause radiation sickness—that is, illness caused by physical and chemical changes in the cells of the body. If a person receives a large dose of radiation, he will die. But if he receives only a small or medium dose, his body will repair itself, and he will get well. A dose received over a short period of time is more damaging than the same dose received over a longer period. Usually the effects of a given dose of radiation are more severe in very young and very old persons, and in those not enjoying good health.

Table 15-1 shows the estimated short-term effects on humans of external exposure to radiation from fallout during a period of less than one week. The total exposure is given in terms of Roentgens (R), a unit for measuring the amount of radiation exposure:

TABLE 15-1. EFFECT OF EXPOSURE TO RADIATION

Exposure	Effects
0–50R	No visible effects.
50–200R	Brief periods of nausea on day of exposure. Fifty percent may experience radiation sickness (nausea); fifty percent may require medical attention; no deaths expected.
200–450R	Most will require medical attention because of serious radiation sickness. Fifty percent deaths within two to four weeks for 450R exposure.
450–600R	Serious radiation sickness; all require medical attention. Death for more than 50 percent within one to three weeks.
Over 600R	Severe radiation sickness. One hundred percent deaths in two weeks.

No special clothing can protect people against gamma radiation, and no special drugs or chemicals can prevent large doses of radiation from causing damage to the cells of the body. However, antibiotics and other medicines are helpful in treating infections that sometimes follow excessive exposure to radiation (which weakens the body's ability to fight infections).

Almost all the radiation that people would absorb from fallout particles would come from particles outside their own bodies. Only simple precautions would be necessary to avoid swallowing the particles, and because of their size (like grains of sand), it would be practically impossible to inhale them.

People exposed to fallout radiation do *not* become radioactive and thereby dangerous to other people. Radiation sickness is not contagious or infectious, and one person cannot "catch it" from another person.

Suggested Procedures

An enemy attack on the United States probably would be preceded by a period of international tension or crisis. This "crisis expectant" period would help alert all citizens to the *possibility* of attack.

Prior to an attack, it is almost certain that enemy preparations would be detected for days before an attack could occur. Moreover, planes and missiles would be detected in time for citizens to get into shelters. Thus, ample warning of an attack could be given. Most certainly there would be an hour or more of warning.

How you received warning of an attack would depend on where you happened to be at that time. The warning might be heard on radio or television, or even by word-of-mouth. Or the first notice of attack might come from the outdoor warning system.

Many U.S. cities and towns have outdoor warning systems, using sirens, whistles, horns, or bells. Although they have been installed mainly to warn citizens of enemy attack, some local governments also use them in connection with natural disasters and other peacetime catastrophes.

Different cities and towns are using their outdoor warning systems in different ways. Most local governments, however, have decided to use a certain signal to warn people of an enemy attack, and a different signal to notify them of a peacetime disaster.

The two "standard" signals that have been adopted in *most* communities are these:

The Attention or Alert Signal. This is used by some local governments to get the attention of citizens in a time of threatened or impending natural disaster, or some other peacetime emergency. The signal itself is a 3- to 5-minute *steady blast* on sirens, whistles, horns, or other devices. In most places, the attention or alert signal means that the local government wants to broadcast on radio or television important information concerning a peacetime disaster.

The Attack Warning Signal. This will be sounded only in an enemy attack. The signal itself is a 3- to 5-minute *wavering sound* on the sirens, or a *series of short blasts* on whistles, horns, or other devices, repeated as deemed necessary. The attack warning signal means that an actual enemy attack against the United States has been detected, and that protective action should be taken immediately. This signal has no other meaning and will be used for no other purpose.

Presently the federal, state, and local governments in the United States are developing a new type of nuclear emergency program to reduce loss of life. This "Crisis Relocation Program" (CRP) calls for the evacuation of civilian populations from cities considered highly vulnerable to nuclear attack. The populations of these cities would move to rural areas within easy automobile driving distance of the cities. Once in the rural areas, the relocated persons would be cared for in residences and other buildings such as schools, churches, office buildings, and warehouses until the crisis ended. Local government officials and volunteers would provide direction and supervision for the displaced people.

Planning and field tests for this program have been conducted by the federal government. The results show that this program is a viable one for the United States—just as it is in the Soviet Union and the Peoples Republic of China. It is very likely, therefore, that approximately 70 million Americans would receive instructions to move from their homes in cities to rural areas during nuclear emergencies. At the same time, other Americans would be instructed to remain in their homes or seek shelter nearby, and perhaps to be prepared to receive and help care for people evacuated from target cities.

If a Blast Occurs without Warning

It is possible—but extremely unlikely—that your first warning of an enemy attack might be the flash of a nuclear explosion in the sky some distance away. Or there might be a flash after warning has been given, possibly while you are on your way to shelter. Under these circumstances, follow these procedures:

- Take cover instantly. If there should be a nuclear flash—especially if you are outdoors and feel warmth at the same time—

take cover instantly in the best place you can find. By getting inside or under something within a few seconds, you might avoid being seriously burned by the heat or injured by the blast wave of the nuclear explosion. If the explosion is some distance away, you might have 5 to 15 seconds before being seriously injured by the heat, and perhaps 15 to 60 seconds before the blast wave arrives. Getting under cover within these time limits might save your life or prevent serious injury. Also, to avoid injuring your eyes, *never look at the flash of an explosion or the nuclear fireball.* You could take cover in any kind of a building, a storm cellar or fruit cellar, a subway station, or tunnel—or even in a ditch or culvert alongside the road, a storm sewer, a cave or outcropping of rock, a pile of heavy materials, a trench or other excavation. Even getting under a parked automobile, bus or train, or a heavy piece of furniture would protect you to some extent. Stay away from windows, so that you can avoid injury from broken glass.

- After taking cover you should lie on your side in a curled-up position, and cover your head with your arms and hands. This would give you some additional protection. If no cover is available, simply lie down on the ground and curl up. The important thing is to avoid being burned by the heat, thrown about by the blast, or struck by flying objects.

- Move to a fallout shelter later. If you protected yourself against the blast and heat waves by instantly taking cover, you could get protection from the radioactive fallout (which would arrive later) by moving to a fallout shelter.

SECTION 2: SURVIVAL TECHNIQUES

Water—the most important survival component. *Courtesy Nelson Wadsworth.*

16. WATER

Water is so abundant in the modern home that it is taken for granted. We expect to see water gushing from taps whenever we turn them on. However, many circumstances, ranging from repair work on a water main to an earthquake or other disaster, can interrupt water service or contaminate the water supply. At times like these, an emergency supply of water is a real asset. Other disasters, such as floods, hurricanes, and wide-ranging fires, can drive us from our homes, destroying everything we own and making survival itself a challenge. This is when finding and decontaminating water can be a major problem.

Home Storage of Emergency Water Supply

The best way to prepare for water shortages is to keep an emergency supply in the home. The great advantage of properly stored water is that its quality can be relied upon even for such needs as baby formula preparation.

Various sources recommend storing a two-week supply of water. The amount often recommended is seven gallons per person for drinking and food preparation, and another seven gallons per person for other limited uses such as hand washing, teeth brushing, and dish washing (total 14 gallons per person for two weeks).

Containers for Water Storage

Glass and plastic containers are commonly used for storing water at home. Containers should be clean and sanitary. Glass containers are breakable and relatively heavy but vapors and gases cannot penetrate them and the amount of chemical that can pass from the glass itself into the water is insignificant. On the other hand, plastic containers are lightweight and substantially more resistant to breakage than glass.

Many kinds of plastic exist. Polyethylene plastic is commonly used for containers of various sizes, including large 57-gallon drums. Take care to use containers made of plastic approved for

117

food contact by the federal Food and Drug Administration. Certain types of plastic containers *not* intended for food contact, such as vinyl plastic water beds, may release undesirable chemicals into stored water. The amount of chemical that approved plastics release into water is negligible.

Generally, polyethylene plastic containers are safe for water storage. A common polyethylene container designed for food contact is the disposable, gallon-size, plastic milk bottle. Liquid chlorine bleach bottles are also made of polyethylene plastic, but the use of such bleach bottles for water storage is *not* recommended because of the potential danger of accidentally drinking bleach instead of water. It is important to prevent small children from identifying containers of a certain shape, size, and color with water if that container normally comes filled with bleach or another hazardous substance. If bleach bottles must be used for water storage, be certain to remove the bleach label and write the word *water* indelibly across the bottle. Insert the water only after the bottles have been thoroughly rinsed with hot water and allowed to dry.

Polyethylene and other plastic containers tend to be permeable to oxygen and carbon dioxide. And certain microorganisms (harmless but undesirable) can grow in stored water if the right combination of oxygen and carbon dioxide exists. Consequently, permeable plastic containers permit such growth. But this problem is easily prevented by starting with clean water and clean containers and treating the water with a small amount of sodium hypochlorite solution (common liquid chlorine bleach, such as Clorox or Purex—see below for details of water disinfection).

The permeability of plastics can be a problem if hydrocarbon vapors are present. Consequently, water stored in plastic containers should not be located near stored gasoline, kerosene, pesticides, or similar substances. Such vapors could permeate the plastic and affect the water.

Polyethylene plastics vary in density, and containers made from them vary in thickness. Both density and thickness affect permeability. For example, the disposable, gallon-size, plastic milk bottle, though made from high density polyethylene, is relatively thin-walled. Thick-walled, high-density polyethylene containers such as drums are significantly *less* permeable to oxygen, carbon dioxide, and hydrocarbon vapors.

Be certain, when selecting a storage container for water, that it has a tight-fitting cap or lid to prevent entrance of contaminants and evaporation of water. Because sunlight has an adverse effect on plastic, water should be stored away from direct exposure to sunlight. Pack containers tightly by wadding newspapers, excelsior, or other packing material between them. This will protect them from damage or shock.

Sanitary Methods of Water Storage

Stored water must be clean water. Use the best water available for storage. Water from systems with an "Approved" or a "Provisionally Approved" rating by a state health agency is recommended.

For long-term storage, water should be sterilized or disinfected. Sterilized water may be stored in glass fruit jars, as follows: Fill clean fruit jars with water, leaving one inch of space at the top of the jar. Place a sterilized lid on each jar and process the water in a boiling water bath as fruit juice is processed. Quart jars should be processed 20 minutes, two-quart jars 25 minutes.

Water stored in plastic or glass containers can be disinfected for long-term storage by treating each gallon with 16 drops of liquid chlorine bleach (Clorox or Purex type bleaches, containing 4 to 6 percent sodium hypochlorite). If no clean eyedropper is available, one-fourth teaspoon of bleach per gallon is recommended. If clean water is used, this treatment will kill organisms in the water and prevent growth of other microorganisms during storage. It will also kill any residual milk bacteria in washed milk bottles; however, milk bottles still must be thoroughly cleansed to prevent sour-milk odor and taste.

Sterilized or disinfected water, stored in clean, food-contact-approved containers with secure lids or caps, should be safe for use even after many years of storage. Be certain to label each container as it is filled so there will be no question about its contents when it is used at a later date. Include the date and information on the method of disinfection used.

Don't Wait to Store Water Supplies

Water to be stored should be drawn into containers *before* it is needed. When a disaster occurs, it may be too late to act. The public water service may already be interrupted or contaminated. Also, if thousands of householders tried to fill water containers at the same time, they would reduce the pressure in the street mains. That would make fire fighting more difficult. Waiting until something happens before you draw and store the water you need could cost you your home, or even your life.

How to Shut Off the Water Service Valve in a Home

To prevent contamination of water in your hot-water heater and other parts of your home's water system, it is vital that you isolate your domestic supply from the water mains. This is done by closing the water service valve. The water service valve usually is located in the basement or just outside the house, often near an outside faucet. Or it may be found in a curb box. Knowing where to find the valve that controls the water service to your home is important, and all members of your family should be acquainted with its location as well. Try the valve to make sure that it works freely. If a tool such as a wrench is needed to operate the valve, be sure you can locate it quickly in an emergency.

Emergency Sources of Liquids in the Home

If you must find additional sources of emergency water, use the utmost care to locate the best water source. The home water heater or toilet tank, for example, may provide good quality water; but even this might be unsafe, especially if the water main has become contaminated.

If you must use water of unknown quality, recognize that no home method of water treatment can *guarantee* safety of the water. Certain water treatment methods described in this chapter can reduce the risks involved, but emergency treatment of water cannot be relied upon to produce the same quality water as a supply of properly stored water. Avoid gadgets that are sold with a claim that they "purify" water.

Water-packed fruit and vegetables are a good source of liquids for drinking purposes in an emergency, provided the containers are undamaged. Fresh fruits are also a good source. However, citrus fruits exposed to radioactive dust or mist should be wiped clean before being squeezed, and other fruits, such as apples and peaches, should be peeled before being eaten.

Another source of good drinking water is your refrigerator. Even if the electricity were shut off, you could drink the water from the melted ice cubes in the trays. All other liquids in the refrigerator would be suitable for drinking if they had not had time to spoil.

If the water in your hot-water heater has not been contaminated from the water main it can be used for drinking. Home hot-water heaters usually have a capacity of 40 or 60 gallons. Before an emergency, keep the hot-water tank free from rust and sediment by opening the drain valve at the bottom of the tank at least once every month until the water runs clean. This procedure will also assure you 40 to 60 gallons of water for washing and cooking purposes. When not under pressure (that is, when the main service valve is closed), all hot-water tanks require venting to the atmosphere before a free flow of water can be obtained from the drain cock. Some are harder to vent than others, depending on the piping arrangement. Most require only the opening of a faucet on the hot water line; others may require that you disconnect the hot-water line from the tank at the coupling usually located at the top of the tank. Know how to obtain water from your tank. When necessary, have the proper tools (pipe wrenches, etc.) handy.

Some water sources may have chemical contamination that makes them unacceptable for drinking. Water beds, for example, usually contain pesticidal chemicals manufactured into the plastic and added to the water to prevent algal, fungal, and bacterial growth. These pesticides and other chemicals that may enter the water from the plastic can render the water unsafe to drink. However, this water may be valuable for such uses as handwashing and laundering.

Emergency Disinfection of Water

Heat Sterilization

Water sterilization by boiling is preferred over any chemical method because disease-causing microorganisms cannot survive the heat of a sterilizing boil. However, there are disadvantages: (1) Fuel is needed, and (2) it takes a long time for the water to boil and then cool. Specifically, the boiling method requires that the water be heated to boiling and held in a vigorous, rolling boil for 5 minutes plus an additional minute for each thousand feet of altitude. It can be used after cooling. Taste may be improved by aerating the water. This can be done by pouring the boiled water back and forth from one clean container to another several times.

Chemical Disinfection

Chemical disinfection of water is an acceptable alternative if boiling is not possible, but only if the water is perfectly clear. Chemical disinfection is less reliable than boiling because many factors affect the disinfection process. For example, the more organic matter in the water, the more chemical is required; and the lower the water temperature, the longer the "contact time" required. (Contact time means the length of time between addition of the disinfecting chemical and use of the water.) Disease-causing organisms, such as viruses can "hide" inside microscopic particles that cause cloudiness in water and can thereby escape the action of the disinfecting chemical. Additional factors include the type of chemical used, the pH of the water, and the types of disease-causing organisms in the water.

Nevertheless, if clear water is given appropriate chemical treatment, it can be rendered safe for use in most emergency situations because of the margin of safety built into chemical disinfection recommendations.

LIQUID BLEACH

Liquid bleach containing between 4 and 6 percent sodium hypochlorite is suitable for home disinfection of water. Each gallon of water should be treated with 16 drops of liquid chlorine bleach, or if no clean eyedropper is available, one-fourth teaspoon of bleach per gallon of water. Treated water should be thoroughly mixed and allowed to stand for 30 minutes before using.

A slight chlorine odor should be detectable in the water. If it is not, repeat the treatment and let the water stand for an additional 15 minutes before using. Treated water may have a slight chlorine taste, but this is additional evidence of safety.

Because liquid chlorine bleach loses strength over time, fresh bleach should be used for water disinfection. If bleach is a year old, the amount used should be doubled. Two-year-old bleach should not be used.

IODINE TABLETS

The U.S. Army has used iodine tablets (Globaline)[1] for emergency disinfection of water for many years. Iodine tablets have the advantage of being more effective against amoebic dysentery cysts[2] and certain other intestinal-parasite cysts[3] than chlorine-based disinfectants such as sodium hypochlorite or Halazone tablets. Sporting goods stores commonly carry these tablets. But be sure that the iodine tablets you buy are fresh; they do lose effectiveness with age. Fresh tablets have a gray color. They have a shelf life of approximately 3 to 5 years unopened. The label should

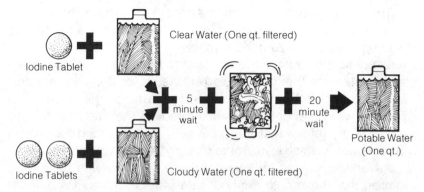

Iodine Tablet

Clear Water (One qt. filtered)

5 minute wait

20 minute wait

Potable Water (One qt.)

Iodine Tablets

Cloudy Water (One qt. filtered)

Figure 16-1. Water-purification procedures. *U.S. Army.*

show an Environmental Protection Agency (EPA) registration number.

Follow instructions on the label, mixing thoroughly and allowing adequate contact time. The iodine tablet should give the water a light yellow to tan color and a slight iodine odor.

HALAZONE TABLETS

Halazone tablets[4]—para-(N,N-,-dichloro-sulfamyl)-benzoic acid— for emergency water disinfection are commonly carried by pharmacies and drug stores. The label should show an Environmental Protection Agency (EPA) registration number. Be certain to note the expiration date, because the shelf-life is only about two years. According to the manufacturer, "It is important that the containers be kept tightly closed to prevent the absorption of moisture from the air. If decomposition of the tablets should occur, they take on a yellowish appearance, have a strong objectionable odor, and, of course, should not be used."[5]

As with iodine tablets, follow the instructions on the label, mixing thoroughly and allowing adequate contact time.

Home Water "Purification" Devices

No home water "purification" device can be fully relied upon to purify grossly contaminated water. In fact, so-called purifiers may promote a false sense of security, because it is certain the "purifier" cannot *produce* water, and it may not be able to decontaminate unsafe water. Under some circumstances, certain "purifiers" have been known to contribute to the water's contamination. Even distillation can produce unacceptable contaminants if the source water contains certain organic chemicals.

The Environmental Protection Agency (EPA) recently issued a statement regarding home-use water-treatment units containing filtering media impregnated with silver: "Bacteriostatic water filtering units are designed to act only on bacteria contained in potable water which is microbiologically safe for drinking. Accordingly, claims will not be accepted for use of these units on polluted well water or raw waters. Moreover, the directions for use must clearly reflect that the product is only intended for use on potable water which is microbiologically safe for drinking."[6]

Advertising claims for some of these water filtering units have implied that they could purify unsafe water, but the EPA emphasized, "Any representation, either directly or by implication, of these products as 'water purifiers' constitutes a false or misleading claim."

In an emergency situation, neither these nor any other home-use device we know of can produce safe drinking water from contaminated water. A home-use device that may reduce one aspect of water contamination may have no effect on a different hazard in the same water.

Finding Water Outside the Home

Water is one of your first and most important needs. You can get along for weeks without food if you have to, but you can't live long without water, especially in hot areas, where a lot of water is lost through sweating. Even in cold areas, your body needs 2 quarts of water a day to maintain efficiency. If you delay drinking, you will have to make it up later on.

Nevertheless, if an emergency demands that you obtain water outside the home, the hazards of using water of unknown quality, including ice and snow, must be weighed against the need. Sterilization or disinfection can reduce the disease hazard of water of unknown quality, but there is no safe method for home decontamination of waters containing hazardous levels of toxic chemicals or radioactive materials. For drinking purposes, chemically or radioactively contaminated water should be avoided entirely. If there is little likelihood that water scavenged from outside the home has been contaminated with hazardous levels of toxic chemicals or radioactive materials, then sterilization by heat or disinfection with chemicals may make it safe for drinking. If the water is cloudy, only heat will destroy all disease-causing organisms.

Collecting Rainwater

Rainwater is generally safe for drinking, with at least one important exception: if a storm passes through the wake of a cloud of
radioactive particles from a nuclear blast, dangerous fallout can
be carried to earth by rain. Of course, you should avoid using water with radioactive contamination.

To collect rainwater, spread out a plastic sheet, blanket, or
cloth over sticks or limbs about six inches above the ground. Create a sag so that the water is funneled to a low spot where a *clean*
container can catch the rain.

Ground Water

When no surface water is available, tap the underground supply.
Be aware, however, that access to this supply depends upon
whether the ground is rocky or made of looser material, such as
clay, gravel, or sand.

In rocky ground look for springs and seepages. Ground water
etches out waterways and caverns in limestone formations. Look
in these caverns for springs. Cold-water springs are safest; warm
water has recently been at the surface and is more likely to be polluted.

Most common rocks, like granite, contain water only in irregular cracks. Scan the hillsides to see where the grass is lush and
green; then dig a ditch just at the base of the greenest area and
wait for water to seep into it. Also look for seepage where a dry
canyon cuts through a layer of porous sandstone.

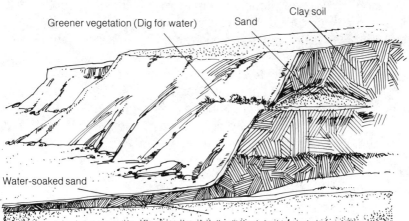

Figure 16-2. Vegetation indicates water. *U.S. Air Force.*

Water is more abundant and easier to find in loose soil than in rocks. Look for springs along valley floors or down along their sloping sides. The flat benches or terraces of land above a river valley usually yield springs or seepages along their bases even when the stream is dry. Dig in the floor of a valley under a steep slope, or dig out a lush green spot where a spring has been flowing during the wet season.

Water moves slowly through clay, but many clays contain strips of sand that may yield springs. Look for a wet place on the surface of a clay bluff and try digging it out. Also try wet spots at the foot of the bluff.

In the coastal areas, you may find some fresh water in dunes above the beach or even on the beach itself, well back from the high line. Look in the hollows between sand dunes for visible water—or dig if the sand seems moist.

Don't waste your time trying to find water by "dowsing" with a forked stick or makeshift divining rod; and don't spend time digging for water unless you recognize some sign that water may be there.

Ice and Snow

In the winter, ice and snow provide water, but fuel is needed to melt them. Never waste fuel melting snow or ice when drinkable water from other sources is available. If short on fuel, you can melt snow in your bare hands or eat an occasional mouthful of clean snow. However, eating ice and snow causes loss of body heat. Therefore, it is best to melt ice and snow before you consume it. It's best to fill up on water at mealtimes once you have melted ice or snow. If fuel is plentiful, try to drink at least 2 quarts of warm water daily instead of cold water or snow.

If the sun is shining, you can melt snow on a dark tarpaulin or any surface that will absorb the sun's heat. Arrange the surface so that meltwater will drain into a hollow or a container.

Use old sea ice for drinking water. It is bluish, has rounded corners, and is free from salt. New sea ice is gray, milky, and hard. Don't drink it. It is as salty as sea water—so salty, in fact, that body fluids must be drawn away to eliminate it. Eventually it will make the kidneys cease functioning.

Water in the Desert

In the desert, your life depends on your water supply. However, don't ration water. People cannot prolong their survival by rationing their water. A general rule: Let your thirst be your guide.

In hot deserts, you need a minimum of a gallon of water a day. If stranded, walk in the cool desert night and you can get about 20 miles on that daily gallon. If walking in daytime heat, you'll be lucky to get 10 miles to the gallon. Whether you sit out your desert survival or walk home, you'll need water.

The only way to conserve your water is to control your sweating. Drink water as you need it, but keep heat out of your body by keeping your clothes on. Clothing helps control sweating by not letting perspiration evaporate so quickly that you get only part of its cooling effect. You may feel more comfortable in the desert without a shirt or pants, because your sweat evaporates fast. But it takes more sweat. Furthermore, you risk getting sunburned— even if you have a good tan. Therefore, wear a hat, use a neck-cloth, and keep your clothes on. Light-colored clothing turns away the heat of the sun and keeps out the hot desert air.

Keep in the shade as much as possible during the day. Desert natives keep their tents open on all sides to allow free circulation of air during the daytime. Sit up a few inches off the ground, if possible; do not lie on the ground. It can be 30°F cooler a foot above the ground than it is right on the ground—a difference that can save a lot of sweat.

Slow motion is better than speed in hot deserts. If you must move about in the heat, you'll last longer on less water if you take it easy. Take a lesson from the Arab: he isn't lazy, he's just living in slow motion, the way the desert makes him live. If you have plenty of water—2 or 3 gallons a day—go ahead and work as hard as you like, and drink as often as you want. In fact, you had better drink more and oftener than you think your thirst requires if you want to stay healthy and efficient.

If you are looking for water along sandy beaches of desert lakes, dig a hole in the first depression behind the first sand dune. Stop digging when you hit wet sand. This first water is fresh or nearly so. If you dig deeper, you may strike salt water. If you find damp sand, dig a hole and wait for water to seep into it. In other places, pick the lowest point between sand dunes and dig 3 to 6 feet. If the sand becomes damp, keep digging until you hit water. In a sand dune belt, search between the outermost dunes of the area, rather than in the middle. (See Figure 16-3.)

In stony desert country, look for dry stream beds. Dig at the lowest point on the outside of a bend in the stream channel. (See Figure 16-4).

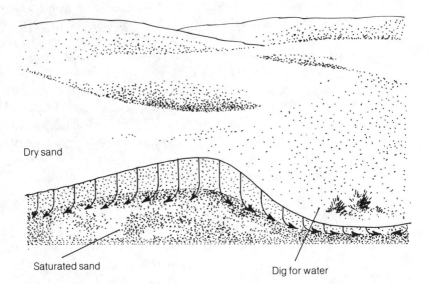

Dry sand

Saturated sand

Dig for water

Figure 16-3. Sand dunes. *U.S. Air Force.*

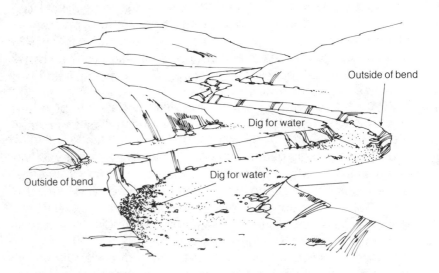

Outside of bend

Dig for water

Outside of bend

Dig for water

Figure 16-4. Dry river bed. *U.S. Air Force.*

In mud flats, during winter, you may find wet mud at the lowest point. To get water, wring out the mud in a piece of cloth. But don't drink the water if it is very salty or soapy-tasting.

In some deserts you may be able to collect dew. Scoop out a hole, line the bottom with a piece of canvas, and fill the basin with pebbles taken from a foot or more underneath the surface. Dew may collect on the rocks and trickle down onto the canvas. Collect the water early in the morning.

Dew sometimes collects on exposed metal surfaces such as the covers of tin cans, as well as on stones or small desert plants. Drain the dew into a cup or mop it up with cloth. It is possible to mop up as much as a quart of dew an hour.

A land solar still consisting of a 6 foot-square transparent plastic sheet stretched over a hole in moist ground may enable you to obtain usable amounts of water. At the center of the hole place a clean container. With stones, anchor the plastic over the hole; then put a small stone on the sheet to make it sag in the middle. Water that condenses on the underside of the plastic will drip from the low point of the sag into the container.

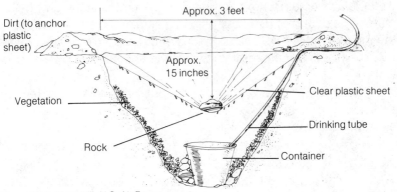

Figure 16-5. Solar still. *U.S. Air Force.*

Water may be obtained from the roots of some desert plants that have their roots near the surface. Cactuslike or succulent plants provide a good source of water. However, do not drink from cactuslike plants that have milky sap—except the barrel cactus of the southwestern United States. And this should be used only as a last resort. Cut off the top of the cactus and smash the pulp within the plant. Catch the liquid in a container. A barrel cactus 3½ feet high will yield a quart of milky juice.

Figure 16-6. Water from the barrel cactus. *U.S. Air Force.*

The presence of vegetation doesn't always mean that surface water is available. But the actions of birds and animals give good clues. The sound of birds chirping in a semiarid brush country often means that water is near. Flocks of birds will circle over a water hole in very dry deserts. Runways and animal trails may lead to water.

"Poison" springs are nonexistent, but waterholes with few or no tracks or plants nearby may have a mineral concentration high enough to cause extreme illness.

Water in Tropical Areas

Water from tropical streams, pools, springs, and swamps is safe to drink only after it has been purified. Discolored or turbid water may be partially cleared by straining it through an improvised filter such as cloth. And you can get water that is almost clear from muddy streams or lakes by digging a hole in sandy soil 1 to 6 feet from the bank. Allow the water to seep in, and then wait for the mud to settle.

In the American tropics, the branches of large trees often support air plants (relatives of the pineapple) whose overlapping leaves may hold rain water. Strain the water through a cloth to eliminate most of the dirt and water insects.

Collect rainwater by digging a hole and lining it with a tarpaulin or a piece of canvas. Catch water from dripping trees by wrapping a clean cloth around a sloping tree, and arranging one end of the cloth to drip into a container.

Animal trails often lead to water. Animals usually go to water at dawn and dark.

Notes

1. Wisconsin Pharmical Co., A Division of Badger Pharmical Inc., New Berlin, WI 53151.

2. Rogers, M. R., A. H. Kaplan, J. J. Vitaliano, and E. Pillion, "Military Individual and Small Group Water Disinfecting Systems: An Assessment," *Military Surgeon* (In Press).

3. Walfe, M. S., "Giardiasis," *Journal of the American Medical Association* 233, no. 13 (1975): 1362–65.

4. Abbott Laboratories, North Chicago, IL 60064.

5. Letters dated 4 November and 16 December 1976 from Patricia Kay Morgan, pharmacist, Pharmaceutical Products Division, Abbott Laboratories, North Chicago, Illinois.

6. "Interim Requirements for Registration of Bacteriostatic Water Treatment Units for Home Use," *Federal Register,* Vol. 41, no. 152 pp. 32778–81, August 5, 1976.

Heat and light. *Courtesy Nelson Wadsworth.*

17. HEAT AND LIGHT

Among the pleasing amenities we are so accustomed to and so dependent upon are abundant heating and lighting. Unlike our forefathers, we do not have to make these things a daily concern; our homes are powered by electricity or gas, for the most part, and control is either automatic or by the mere flick of a switch.

However, electrical power and natural gas are very often among the first services interrupted during natural disasters. To prepare for such emergencies, it is wise to plan ahead for alternate sources of heat and light for your home. Moreover, for those disasters that could leave you homeless or stranded in a wilderness area, it is best to be prepared with a knowledge of survival techniques for building fires. In most survival circumstances, a fire is necessary for keeping warm and dry, for cooking, purifying water, and signaling.

Alternative Heating for Your Home

In an emergency the ways to heat your home vary from elaborate systems to simple, survival-type burners. None but the most carefully planned system can provide the comfort that most people are used to, but any source of heat that is reliable in an emergency will be better than nothing at all.

When the regular heating system fails during cold weather, the family should close off much of the house and limit itself to one or two rooms. Trying to heat the whole house would be difficult, if not impossible, and would waste fuel. The kitchen is the best choice as a family room, because it can be warmed by the heat given off while food is cooking.

Fireplaces and Stoves

Masonry fireplaces are both inefficient and relatively expensive. However, if a masonry fireplace already exists in your home, there are ways to increase its heat efficiency:
- Heat-circulating metal units that insert into the present firebox are available. In theory, the air heated by one of these units

133

rises to form swirllike currents beneath a V-shaped duct. This delay in the air flow causes a transfer of heat energy that otherwise would have gone up the flue.

- You can use a hollow grate that serves not only to hold the burning wood but also to set up convection currents as well. Cool air is sucked into the bottom ends of the tubes, warmed in the middle, and discharged through the openings on top.
- You can install a modern woodburning stove (modified Franklin stove) in your fireplace opening, using the existing chimney. There are many kinds of these stoves available. They are airtight and have automatic draft controls that are efficient because they draw smaller quantities of air.

If no fireplace exists, free-standing metal fireplaces and Franklin-type stoves are possibilities. These units heat by both radiation from the fire and some contact heating of the air by the metal hood and exposed chimney pipes. And because this type of heating unit usually cannot be backed against a wall (they commonly require two feet of clearance from combustible walls but can be placed closer to a masonry surface), heating in all four directions is an important benefit.

Prefabricated fireplaces of many different designs are also available. These units typically have, on the sides and bottom, inlets that draw air into a chamber surrounding the steel jacket of the firebox. There the air is warmed. Then, through ducts at the top, the air is discharged into the room.

If you do use a fireplace, make sure the room is well ventilated, the damper open, and the flue unobstructed before lighting your fire. Poor ventilation will make the fireplace smoke. Avoid burning wet or green wood. Place a screen in front of your grate to catch any sparks that fly. Keep a fire extinguisher handy, and keep other combustibles at a distance. Never use flammable liquids indoors to light your fire.

You don't have to have a roaring fire to have a good fire. Generally, no more than four logs are needed. Adjust the logs and maintain the flames by pushing the ends into the flame from time to time. Rake coals toward the front of the grate before adding new logs. Add new logs at the rear of the fireplace; there they will reflect light and heat into the room.

Ashes under the grate are important because they form a bed for glowing coals that drop through the grate. They concentrate heat and direct drafts of air up to the base of the fire. But don't let ashes accumulate higher than an inch or two below the grate. A greater accumulation can ruin andirons and block the flow of air to the fire. You can check the flaming fire by covering the burning logs with excess ashes; a fire "banked" with ashes in this way will hold glowing coals for 8 to 10 hours, making it easier to rekindle the flames.

Camp Stoves

Camp stoves that burn either white gas or propane can be very useful and very easily operated. Propane is more expensive, but it is also more convenient to use. However, when the demand is greatest, the supply of standard propane cylinders may dwindle. A refillable bulk tank initially costs more but allows long-term savings. During an emergency, supplies of white gasoline may also run short. Thus it is best to keep a supply on hand.

Gasoline and propane stoves both consume oxygen; therefore, using them indoors in a completely closed kitchen or bedroom is hazardous.

Canned Heat

Canned-heat burners may be used safely indoors, except in shelters where burning fuel may deplete the oxygen supply or expose the occupants to carbon monoxide poisoning.

To use canned heat properly, first remove the paper label from around the can. Pry off the cover and touch a lighted match to the can's contents. Never blow the flame out. To extinguish it, slide the cover on upside down. Wait for the can to cool, turn the cover right side up, and press down. Prevent canned heat from evaporating by keeping the cover on tight when not in use.

Store at least one canned-heat stove and 14 large cans of canned heat per stove.

Heat-Tab Stoves

These were invented for use by backpackers. They are very small and designed for one-man use.

Charcoal Grills

Charcoal grills are common to most households. Cooking is easy, there is the advantage of a nonflame heat source, and charcoal briquets are safe and easy to store.

However, adequate ventilation is a must because burning charcoal releases carbon monoxide. Some modern homes, especially those with electric heating, are constructed so airtight than an air vent may have to be installed, or a window opened. Never use charcoal in a camper or trailer; if you do, you will risk carbon monoxide poisoning.

Fuels for Storage

An alternative heating source would be useless without fuel. Therefore, it is imperative that attention be given to fuel storage *before* the need arises. For example, most wood will burn poorly at best when freshly cut; the surest way of having dry, usable wood is to obtain it several months before using it. Other fuels may be scarce or impossible to deliver when an emergency strikes.

Wood

The heat that a fireplace log produces depends on the concentration of woody material, resin, water, and ash. Because woods are of different compositions, they ignite at different temperatures and give off different amounts of heat; therefore, it is best to mix light and heavy woods to achieve the ideal fire.

Softwoods such as pine, spruce, and fir are easy to ignite because they are resinous. They burn rapidly with a hot flame. However, a fire built entirely of softwoods burns out quickly. This is fine if you want a quick warming fire or a fire that will burn out before you go to bed. But for a longer-lasting fire it is best to add heavier hardwoods such as ash, beech, birch, maple, and oak. These dense species burn less vigorously than softwoods and with a shorter flame. Oak gives the most uniform and shortest flame and produces steady, glowing coals. Burning green or wet or highly resinous wood produces considerable wood tar and several associated "smoke" products. These tars and extracts may coat the chimney flue and could result in a chimney fire if ignited.

Some resinous woods are best used as stove woods or only with caution in the fireplace. Hemlock, larch, spruce, and juniper all contain moisture pockets in the wood. Upon heating, trapped gases and water vapor build pressure in these pockets and "pop" violently. This is another reason for reducing moisture content as much as possible before burning any firewood.

TABLE 17-1. RATINGS FOR FIREWOOD

	Relative amount of heat	Is it easy to ignite?	Is it easy to split?	Does it have heavy smoke?	Does it pop or throw sparks?	General rating and remarks
Hardwood Trees						
Apple, ash, beech, birch, dogwood, hard maple, hickory, locust, mesquite, oak, Pacific madrone, pecan	High	No	Medium	Little	Yes, when poked	Excellent
Alder, cherry, soft maple, walnut	Medium	Medium	Yes	Little	Little	Good
Elm, gum, sycamore	Medium	Medium	No	Medium	Little	Fair—contains too much water when green
Aspen, basswood, cotton, yellow poplar	Low	Yes	Yes	Medium	Little	Fair—but good for kindling
Softwood Trees						
Douglas fir, southern yellow pine	Medium	Yes	Yes	Yes	Little	Good but smoky
Cypress, redwood	Low	Yes	Yes	Medium	Little	Fair
Eastern red cedar, western red cedar, white cedar	Low	Yes	Yes	Medium	Yes	Fair—excellent for kindling
Eastern white pine, ponderosa pine, sugar pine, western white pine, true firs	Low	Yes	Yes	Medium	Little	Fair—good kindling
Larch, tamarack	Medium	Yes	Yes	Yes	Yes	Fair
Spruce	Low	Yes	Yes	Medium	Yes	Fair—but good for kindling when dry

U.S. Forest Service, USDA.

Newspaper Logs

Usable "logs" can be made from newspapers. After all, newsprint is nothing more than treated wood fiber.

Soak newspapers overnight in water, or soak them for two hours in water to which one cup of laundry detergent has been added. Roll the newspapers onto a rod (round piece of wood one inch in diameter). Remove the rod from the center of the log. Tie each log with string, and stand the rolls on end to dry.

Use newspaper logs as you would regular wood logs.

Coal

In some parts of the U.S., coal is easily available. Coal should be stored in a dark location and away from air: in a covered hole or pit (line pit with plastic or place coal in bags or barrels), in a basement room, or in a coal bin or shed.

Fire Making in the Outdoors

Under many circumstances in the outdoors, fire is not only welcome but essential. A candle in a tin can makes a simple heater for a small shelter. In the open, a larger fire or fires may be needed. Whatever your needs—warmth, cooking, signaling—consider the following tried and proven advice.

Kindling and Fuel

Most fuels cannot be started burning directly from a match. Tinder, kindling, and fuel are generally required.

Tinder is very fine, dry material that can make a flame from a spark or pick up the flame from a match. When you have matches, tinder may be dry twigs, fine shavings, or a "fuzz stick." But starting fires without matches requires very dry powdered wood or finely shredded dry bark; lint from unravelled cloth, cotton, twine, rope, or first-aid gauze bandage; fuzzy or woolly material scraped from plants; fine bird feathers or birds' nests. Tinder must be bone dry. Once prepared, it should be kept in a waterproof container for future use and exposed to the sun on dry days. Adding a little powdered charcoal will improve it. Collect good tinder wherever you can find it.

Kindling is small, dry fuel that will take flame from tinder and burn hot enough to ignite regular fuel. Good natural kindling materials are thin sticks or dry wood, dry bark, wood shavings, twigs, ferns, and dead, upright grass straw. If sticks are used for kindling, split them and cut long, thin shavings, leaving the shavings attached. Crumpled paper is also good kindling.

For fuel, use dry standing dead wood and dry dead branches. Dead wood is easy to split and break: simply pound it on a rock. To split logs, whittle hardwood wedges and drive them into cracks in the log; split wood burns more easily. The inside of fallen tree trunks and large branches may be dry even if the outside is wet; use the heart of the wood. Even when wet, though, the resinous pitch in pine knots or dried stumps will ignite readily. Low, dead, needle-bearing branches of standing trees are also good fuel. If a small branch snaps when broken in two, it is dead and dry.

Almost anywhere, you can find green wood that will burn, especially if it is finely split. In treeless areas, you can find other natural fuels, such as dry grass (which you can twist into bunches), dried animal dung, animal fats and bones, and sometimes even coal, oil shale, or oil sand lying on the surface. Look for any woody bush or shrub; burn roots as well as stems. On the coasts, look for driftwood.

Always keep firewood and kindling dry under shelter, and use your fire to dry out damp kindling and wood for future use. Save some of your best kindling and fuel for making a quick fire in the morning.

Preparing a Fireplace

Prepare the location of your fire carefully. Clear away leaves, twigs, moss, and dry grass so that you don't start a grass or forest fire. If the ground is dry, scrape down to bare dirt. If the fire must be built on snow, ice, or wet ground, build a platform of logs or flat stones. Don't build a fire under a snow-covered tree—snow may fall and put out the fire.

To get the most warmth and to protect your fire from wind, build it against a rock or a wall of logs that will serve as a reflector to direct the heat into your shelter. Cooking fires should be walled in by logs or stones, not only to concentrate the heat but also to provide a platform for your cooking pot.

Starting Your Fire

There are many ways to build a fire. The basic principle is that you first light easily ignitable tinder, which in turn ignites the kindling, which in turn ignites the larger firewood.

FIRE MAKING WITH MATCHES

After preparing your fireplace, gather enough fuel to start a fire and keep it going. Make sure your matches, kindling, and fuel are dry.

Place a small amount of tinder in the fireplace, and place above this a scattering of small twigs or light bark. Next, arrange above this a small amount of larger twigs or split softwood kindling in a low pyramid, close enough together that flames can burn from one piece to another. Leave a small opening for lighting the tinder.

Small pieces of wood or other fuel can be laid gently on the kindling before you light the fire, or they can be added after the kindling begins to burn. A tepee formation of kindling and small branches will ease your fire through early combustion stages until the logs are aglow.

Save matches by using a candle to light the fire, if you have one. If you have no candle, use a "shave stick," or make a fagot of thin, dry twigs tied loosely together. Shield your match from the wind and light the candle or fagot; apply the flame to the lower windward side of your tinder, shielding it from wind as you do so.

When the fire has gathered strength, lay on smaller pieces of wood and then larger ones. Don't smother the fire by crushing down kindling with heavy wood. Place logs close together; the narrow air spaces between them promote better drafts, and the heat reflected between adjacent surfaces aids in raising and maintaining combustion temperatures.

Don't build your fire too big. Small fires require less fuel and are easier to control, and their heat can be concentrated. In cold weather, small fires arranged in a circle around an individual are much more effective than one large fire.

To make a fire last overnight, place large logs over it so that the fire will burn into the heart of the logs. When a good bed of coals has been formed, cover it lightly with ashes and then dry earth. In the morning the fire will still be smoldering.

Be sure that you don't waste your matches by trying to light a poorly prepared fire, and don't build unnecessary fires. Practice primitive methods of making fires before all your matches are gone.

FLINT AND STEEL

This is the easiest and most reliable way of making a fire without matches. If you have no flint, look for a piece of hard rock from which you can strike sparks. If the rock breaks or scars when struck with steel, throw it away and find another.

To make a fire, hold your hands close over dry tinder; using a knife blade or other small piece of steel, strike the flint with a sharp, scraping, downward motion so that sparks will fall in the center of the tinder. When the tinder begins to smolder, fan it gently into a flame. Then transfer the blazing tinder to your kindling pile, or move the kindling gradually to the tinder.

Figure 17-1. Fire making with flint and steel. *U.S. Air Force.*

METAL MATCH

A metal match is waterproof, fireproof, nontoxic, and durable. It will light one to three thousand fires, depending on its size.

It is fast and simple to use: shave or scrape small pieces of metal from the match with the back of a knife, a sharp rock, or any other hard object. These particles are accumulated in a small area of tinder, then ignited with a spark from the match.

FRICTION

There are many methods of making fire by friction (e.g., bow and drill, fire plough, and fire thong), but all require practice. If you are proficient in one of these methods, use it; but remember that flint and steel will give you the same results with less work.

ELECTRIC SPARK

If you have a live storage battery, direct a spark onto the tinder by scratching the ends of wires together to produce an arc.

STEEL WOOL AND FLASHLIGHT BATTERIES

Use steel wool (a scouring pad, for example) and two flashlight batteries. Hold the two cells in one fist, the top of one touching the bottom of the other in a firm contact. Shred out the steel wool and tuck one end under the bottom cell. Touch the upper end of the steel wool to the contact pole of the upper battery. The steel wool will glow and burn hotly. Place the burning steel wool in tinder and fan into flames.

Figure 17-2. Fire making with burning glass. *U.S. Air Force.*

BURNING GLASS

Any convex lens can be used in bright sunlight to concentrate the sun's rays on tinder and start it burning.

Emergency Lighting

Flashlights

According to one manufacturer of portable lighting equipment, more than 90 percent of all households have a flashlight; but in an emergency, people in a typical household will not be able to locate it. Even if it is found, the batteries may have lost their energy.

Batteries wear down even when not used, and removing them from a flashlight will not extend battery life. "Shelf life" is the time a battery can be stored at 70°F before it loses 10 percent of its energy output. The shelf life depends on the type of battery chosen.

Carbon-zinc cells are cheapest and can be used for most low-demand purposes. They have a shelf life of about nine months, at which time they will produce about two hours of continuous life. Alkaline cells are more expensive, but their shelf life is about twice that of carbon-zinc cells and they will give about ten hours of continuous light.

Whatever the choice of flashlight batteries, check them periodically (about every three months) and replace them whenever necessary.

Battery-powered lanterns (either 6-volt or 12-volt) will generally provide light for 24 to 86 hours. A fluorescent battery lantern is also available.

Chemical Light

The Cyalume Chemical Light (made by American Cyanamid Company) is a plastic tube about seven inches long containing two chemicals, one in a glass vial. Under normal conditions the tubes may be stored for up to four years. To activate the light, the tube is flexed so that the glass vial breaks and the chemicals mix. The luminous yellow green light will last for 8 to 10 hours. The light is flameless, cool, windproof, waterproof, and nontoxic. It cannot be turned off once activated, and it must be discarded when dead.

Candles

Candles served the pioneers well and can do likewise in case of a power outage. Candles are easily lit and relit.

Bob R. Zabriskie, in his book *Family Storage* (Bookcraft, Inc.: Salt Lake City, Utah, 1974), indicates the following burning times for candles of different sizes:

¾ inch diameter, 4 inches tall—will burn 2½ hours
⅞ inch diameter, 4 inches tall—will burn 5 hours
2 inches square, 4 inches tall—will burn 28 hours
2 inches square, 9 inches tall—will burn 63 hours

Lanterns

A single-mantle camping lantern will produce about as much light as a 75-watt light bulb and will burn about two ounces of propane or three of gasoline per hour. A double-mantle lantern can produce about 20 percent more light and uses about three ounces of propane or five ounces of gasoline an hour.

Kerosene lamps also provide good light, though safety precautions should be exercised. (See Table 17-2 for comparative rates of fuel consumption.)

TABLE 17-2. SOME FUEL-CONSUMPTION RATES

Fuel	Amount or size	Burning Time	Comments
White gas, lanterns—			
two mantle	2 pints	10 to 12 hrs.	
single mantle	2 pints	16 to 18 hrs.	
Kerosene lanterns	1 quart	45 hours	One wick lantern
Candles	¾" × 4"	2 hrs. 20 min.	
	⅞" × 4"	5 hrs.	
	2" sq × 9" tall	63 hours	Based on 4½ hours burning time per day
Heaters	5 quarts	18 to 20 hrs.	8,000 BTU
Catalytic heater	3 quarts	12 hrs.	5,000 BTU
(white gas)	2 quarts	18 to 20 hrs.	3,500 BTU
Stoves, two-burner	3½ pint		
	aerosol can	4 hrs.	Using both burners
	white gas	4 hrs.	Using standard setting
	20-lb. trailer tank	120 hrs.	Stove
		200 hrs.	Lantern

Barbara G. Salsbury, Just in Case: A Manual of Home Preparedness, Bookcraft, Inc.: Salt Lake City, 1975. By permission.

Generators for Home Use

Another source of emergency electrical power is a car's generator or alternator. A temporary 12-volt trouble lamp can be plugged into a car's cigarette lighter socket, and several companies sell converters that will supply enough current to power lights, radios, and small appliances. However, these converter kits will not run refrigerators, freezers, furnaces, or other large appliances. But auxiliary alternators designed for use in addition to the car's standard alternator can power large appliances.

The small, gasoline-powered portable auxiliary generator is more efficient than the automobile source; and though it is more costly, it is less expensive to run. Rural dwellers and owners of recreational vehicles and vacation cabins may have one already. Emergency generators have been used by hospitals and industry for many years. Available now is a gasoline-powered standby generator for home use, capable of producing 300 to 5,000 watts—enough energy to run a home heating furnace, refrigerator, and a limited number of lights and other electrical appliances.

But even the best auxiliary unit has much less capacity than normal service, so you will have to pick and choose among things you want to use.

To be sure your home unit will start when you need it, test it periodically, summer and winter. Before operating the machine, you must either switch off the outside utility line to your house or have a safety device installed—so that electricity doesn't feed back and jeopardize someone working on the power lines. Installation by a licensed electrician is recommended.

One final note: many home units in operation sound like a gasoline-powered lawn mower.

Food storage: *Courtesy Nelson Wadsworth.*

18. FOOD

When the first terrible effects of a disaster have passed and lives are no longer in immediate peril, other concerns come to the fore. Not the least of these is the concern for adequate supplies of safe and palatable food. A supply of food stored away for just such emergencies would be welcome and virtually priceless if it were needed badly. Moreover, a disaster that left people to rely on their own resources for extended periods would also demonstrate the great value of knowing how to find and prepare food in the wilds. This chapter offers the reader a basic knowledge of food storage techniques and ways to survive using foods found in nature.

FOOD STORAGE

The Emergency Food Supply

As a precaution against disasters, Civil Defense preparedness authorities recommend that you purchase and store an emergency supply of food sufficient for at least two weeks.

These stockpile foods should be in cans, jars, or sealed paper or plastic containers. Select foods that will last for months without refrigeration and that can be eaten with little or no cooking.

The needs and preferences of family members are important to consider as you prepare your list of emergency foods. Buy foods that you and your family know. As many of your stored foods as possible should be useful in your normal diet, so that you can use and replace your reserve supply and thereby be sure of its freshness. Suggested foods are listed in Table 18-1.

Do not buy more food than you have cool, dry, secure storage space for. The amounts indicated in Table 18-1 will supply the calories needed by one adult for two weeks. If your family consists of four adults, store four times the amounts suggested. Teenagers are likely to eat more than an adult; younger children need less. If necessary, include special kinds of milk and strained, chopped, or other specially prepared foods required for infants, elderly persons, and others on limited diets. By including foods from each of the eight groups listed, you can assure your family a reasonably nutritious diet.

Whenever possible, choose cans and jars in sizes that will fill your family's needs for only one meal. This is especially important for meat, poultry, fish, vegetables, evaporated milk, and other foods that deteriorate rapidly after a container is opened.

If your home freezer is located in your basement or where you would have safe access to it after an emergency, you might count foods in it as some of your reserve supply. Food spoilage in a well-filled, well-insulated home freezer does not begin until several days after power goes off. Foods in large freezers will keep longer than food in small freezers. Once the freezer has been opened, foods should be used as promptly as possible.

TABLE 18-1. GUIDE FOR TWO-WEEK FOOD SUPPLY

| Kind of Food | Amount per Person | | Remarks |
	One Day	Two Weeks	
Milk	Equivalent of 2 glasses (fluid)	Equivalent of 7 quarts (fluid)	Each of the following is the equivalent of 1 quart of fluid milk: ■ Evaporated milk: three 6-ounce cans; one 14½-ounce can. ■ Nonfat dry milk or whole dry milk: 3 to 3½ ounces.
Canned meat, poultry, fish, cooked dry beans, and peas	2 servings	28 servings (8 to 9 pounds)	Amounts suggested for one serving of each food are as follows: ■ Canned meat, poultry: 2 to 3 ounces. ■ Canned fish: 2 to 3 ounces. ■ Canned mixtures of meat, poultry, or fish with vegetables, rice, macaroni, spaghetti, noodles, or cooked dry beans: 8 ounces. ■ Condensed soups containing meat, poultry, fish, or dry beans or dry peas: one-half of a 10½-ounce can.

| Kind of Food | Amount per Person | | Remarks |
	One Day	Two Weeks	
Fruits and vegetables	3 to 4 servings	42 to 56 servings (about 21 pounds, canned)	Amounts suggested for one serving of each food are as follows: ■ Canned juices: 4 to 6 ounces, single strength. ■ Canned fruit and vegetables: 4 ounces. ■ Dried fruit: 1½ ounces.
Cereals and baked goods	3 to 4 servings	42 to 56 servings (5 to 7 pounds)	Amounts suggested for one serving of each food are as follows (selection depends on extent of cooking possible): ■ Cereal: ready-to-eat puffed: ½ ounce. Ready-to-eat flaked: ¾ ounce. Other ready-to-eat cereal: 1 ounce. Uncooked (quick-cooking): 1 ounce. ■ Crackers: 1 ounce. ■ Cookies: 1 ounce. ■ Canned bread, steamed puddings, and cake: 1 to 2 ounces. ■ Flour mixes: 1 ounce. ■ Flour: 1 ounce. ■ Macaroni, spaghetti, noodles: Dry: ¾ ounce. Cooked, canned: 6 ounces.
Spreads for bread and crackers	According to family practices		Examples: Cheese spreads. Peanut and other nut butters. Jam, jelly, marmalade, preserves. Syrup, honey. Apple and other fruit butters. Relish, catsup, mustard.
Fats and vegetable oil	Up to 1 pound or 1 pint		Amount depends on extent of cooking possible. Kinds that do not require refrigeration.
Sugars, sweets, and nuts	1 to 2 pounds		Sugar, hard candy, gum, nuts, instant puddings.
Miscellaneous	According to family practices and extent of cooking possible		Examples: Cocoa (instant). Dry cream product (instant). Bouillon products. Flavored beverage powders. Salt and pepper. Flavoring extracts, vinegar. Soda, baking powder.

U.S. Dept. of Agriculture.

Sample Meal Plans

Sample meal plans are presented in Tables 18-2 and 18-3. These plans suggest the kinds of meals you could serve from the foods shown in Table 18-1. Half the menus require no cooking facilities. The other meals require facilities for heating water or food but not for any extended cooking.

If you have provided a sufficient variety of canned foods in your reserve supply, it is possible to have reasonably well-balanced meals. However, because of limited space and in order to use fewer dishes, it may be more practical to serve a limited variety of foods at each meal but make the servings more generous.

TABLE 18-2. SAMPLE MEAL PLANS—NO COOKING FACILITIES

First Day	Second Day	Third Day
Morning		
Citrus fruit juice[1]	Fruit juice[1]	Grapefruit segments[1]
Ready-to-eat cereal	Corned beef hash[1]	Ready-to-eat cereal
Milk	Crackers	Vienna sausage[1]
Crackers	Spread	Milk, cold beverage[2]
Peanut butter or other spread	Milk, cold beverage[2]	
Noon		
Spaghetti with meat sauce[1]	Baked beans[1]	Chile con carne with beans[1]
Green beans[1]	Brown bread[1]	crackers
Crackers	Tomatoes[1]	Fruit[1]
Spread	Fruit[1]	Cookies
Milk, cold beverage[2]	Milk, cold beverage[2]	Milk, cold beverage[2]
Between Meals		
Fruit-flavored drink or fruit drink	Milk	Tomato juice
Night		
Lunch meat[1]	Pork and gravy[1]	Sliced beef[1]
Sweet potatoes[1]	Corn[1]	Macaroni and cheese[1]
Applesauce[1]	Potatoes[1]	Peas and carrots[1]
Milk, cold beverage[2]	Instant pudding	Crackers
Candy	Fruit juice[1]	Milk, cold beverage[2]

[1]canned
[2]instant

U.S. Dept. of Agriculture.

150

TABLE 18-3. SAMPLE MEAL PLANS—LIMITED COOKING FACILITIES

First Day	Second Day	Third Day
Morning		
Citrus fruit juice[1]	Citrus fruit juice[1]	Prunes[1]
Ready-to-eat cereal	Hot cereal (quick-	Ready-to-eat cereal
Milk	cooking)	Milk
Cocoa or hot beverage[2]	Milk	Crackers
	Cocoa or hot beverage[2]	Cheese
		Cocoa or hot beverage[2]
Noon		
Vegetable soup[1]	Beef-and-vegetable stew[1]	Chile con carne with
Potato salad[1]	Green beans[1]	beans[1]
Crackers	Crackers	Tomatoes[1]
Ham spread[1]	Peanut butter	Crackers
Milk	Milk	Cocoa or hot beverage[2]
Between Meals		
Fruit-flavored drink or fruit drink	Tomato juice[1]	Fruit-flavored drink or fruit drink
Night		
Beef and gravy[1]	Tuna fish[1], cream of	Lunch meat[1]
Noodles[1]	celery soup[1], mixed sweet	Hominy[1]
Peas and carrots[1]	pickles—combined in one	Applesauce[1]
Instant pudding	dish	Cookies
Cocoa or hot beverage[2]	Fruit[1]	Cocoa or hot beverage[2]
	Cookies	
	Cocoa or hot beverage[2]	
[1]canned		
[2]instant		

U.S. Dept. of Agriculture

The Basic Foods for Long-Term Storage

Many authorities suggest that, in addition to a short-term emergency supply, families should store a full year's supply of food beginning with the "basic four": milk, grains, sugar or honey, and salt. Long-term home storage of food should begin with these basic items, which will sustain life in an emergency. Later, when these have been stored in adequate amounts, consideration could be given to adding a wider variety of foods that the family normally eats.

How much to store? The following quantities of each basic item are recommended for storage to sustain an average adult for one year:

Grains (wheat, rice, other cereal grains)	300 lbs
Powdered milk (nonfat)	75 lbs
Sugar or honey	60 lbs
Salt	5 lbs
Fat or oil	20 lbs
Dried legumes	60 lbs

These items, used exclusively, provide approximately 2,300 calories a day. The quantities may be reduced as other foods are added. These basic foods should be supplemented with foods that supply adequate amounts of vitamin C and A.

To the basic foods others may be added according to availability and individual taste. Fresh taro or sweet potato, live pigs, chickens, and fish might be considered as basic items in areas where it is difficult to store food.

Rotating Your Stored Foods

It is a good idea to draw regularly on your food stockpile, using foods while they are still nutritious and palatable. As food items are used, replace them with fresh supplies. Place fresh supplies at the back of the stockpile, keeping older supplies in front. You may want to label cans and containers with the date of purchase and the approximate date when the particular item should be replaced.

Table 18-4 suggests replacement periods for the kinds of food listed in Table 18-1.

Eating quality was the first consideration in setting these maximum replacement periods. Many food items will be acceptable for a much longer period if storage temperatures do not usually exceed 70°F. Most of the foods suggested in Table 18-4 would be safe to use after longer storage periods.

Canned foods are generally safe to eat as long as the seal of the can is not broken. Food spoilage may have occurred if a can has bulging ends, is leaking, or if, when the can is opened, there is spurting liquid, off-odor, or mold on the food.

When food in glass containers becomes spoiled, the cover may bulge or the container may show leakage of the food through the broken seal. Gas bubbles, cloudiness, and films of growth that can be seen through the glass may indicate bacterial growth.

If the seal has broken on jars of baby food, the "safety button" in the center of the lid will be pushed upward instead of drawn downward.

TABLE 18-4. REPLACEMENT PERIODS FOR FOODS LISTED IN TABLE 18-1

Use within 6 Months
Evaporated milk
Dried fruit, in metal
  container
Dry crisp crackers, in
  metal container
Gum

Use within 1 Year
Nonfat dry or whole dry
  milk, in metal container
Canned meat, poultry, fish
Mixtures of meat, vege-
  tables, and cereal pro-
  ducts, in sealed cans
  or jars

Canned condensed meat-
  and-vegetable soups
Dehydrated soups in
  metal container
Canned fruits, fruit juices,
  and vegetables.
Cereal:
  Ready-to-eat cereals, in
    metal container
  Uncooked cereal
  (quick-cooking or
  instant), in metal con-
  tainer
Hydrogenated fats, vege-
  table oils
Sweets and nuts:

Hard candy
Nuts, canned
Instant puddings
Miscellaneous:
  Cocoa (instant), hot
    beverages
  Dry cream products
  (instant)

  Bouillon products
  Flavored beverage
  products
  Flavoring extracts
  Soda, baking powder

May be Stored Indefinitely
Sugar
Salt

U.S. Dept. of Agriculture.

Food from containers showing any signs of food spoilage should be discarded immediately *without tasting.*

Where and How to Store Food

Generally there is a place in the home that meets the requirements for maintaining the quality of the stored products. It should be cool (not above 70°F and not below freezing), dark, away from dust, smoke, water pipes, moisture or steam. It should be free from any products such as kerosene, paints, oil, and other substances that might affect the flavor or odor of food. It should be well ventilated and clean.

Do not place food or food containers directly on cement floors. Place slats of lumber under the food to prevent moisture damage.

Food in paper boxes can be protected from rodents and insects by storing the boxes in tightly closed cans or other metal containers; leave the foods in their original boxes. Keeping these foods in metal containers also extends the length of time they can be stored. Many different kinds of plastic, metal, and glass containers are available.

For a rather complete list of common foods and their shelf life, refer to Appendix 3: "Storage Chart," and Table 18-5.

TABLE 18-5. HOME STORAGE CHART: FRESH VEGETABLES

		Storage Conditions		
Vegetables	Where to Store	Temp. (°F)	Humidity	Storage Period
Beans and peas, dried	Any cool, dry place	32–40	Dry	Many Years
Beets	Storage cellar or pit	32–40	Moist	Fall-winter
Cabbage	Storage cellar or pit	32–35	Moist	Fall-winter
Carrots	Storage cellar or pit	32–40	Moist	Fall-winter
Celery	Roots in soil in storage cellar	32–40	Moist	Fall-winter
Onions	Any cool, dry place	As near 32 as possible	Dry	Fall-winter
Parsnips	Leave in ground or put in storage cellar	32–40	Moist	Fall-winter
Potatoes	Storage cellar or pit	45–48	Moist	Fall-winter
Pumpkin, winter squash	Unheated room or basement	55–60	Dry	Fall-winter
Rutabagas	Storage cellar or pit	32–40	Moist	Fall-winter
Sweet Potatoes	Unheated room or basement	55–60	Dry	Fall-winter
Tomatoes (green or white)	Unheated room or basement	55–60	Dry	1–6 weeks
Turnips	Storage cellar or pit	32–40	Moist	Fall-winter
Fruits				
Most apples McIntosh, Yellow Newton and Rhode Island Greening	Fruit storage cellar	30–32	Moist	Fall-winter
	Fruit storage cellar	35–38	Moist	Fall-winter
Grapes	Fruit storage cellar	31–32	Moist	4-6 weeks
Pears	Fruit storage cellar	30–31	Moist	Fall-winter
Peaches	Fruit storage cellar	32	Moist	2 weeks
Apricots	Fruit storage cellar	32	Moist	2 weeks

U.S. Dept. of Agriculture

TABLE 18-6. SOME AVAILABLE VARIETIES OF DEHYDRATED AND FREEZE-DRIED FOODS

Fruits	Vegetables	Juice	Dairy Products	Meat
Apples (d or f)	Beans, green	Crystals (d or	Butter, pow-	Beef chunks
Apricots (d or	(d or f)	f)	dered (d)	(f)
f)	Beets (d or f)	Lemon	Buttermilk (d)	Beef, diced (f)
Bananas	Carrots (d or f)	Orange	Cheese, pow-	Beef patties (f)
flakes (d)	Celery (d or f)	Grapefruit	dered (d)	Beef steak (f)
slices (f)	Corn (d or f)	Grape	Cottage	Chicken,
Dates (d)	Green peppers		cheese (f)	chunks (f)
Figs (d)	(d or f)		Cream, pow-	Chicken,
Fruit Cocktail	Onions (d)		dered sour	diced (f)
(d or f)	Peas (d or f)		(d)	
Peaches (d or f)	Potatoes (d)		Cream, pow-	
Pears (d or f)	Soup Blend		dered sweet	
Pineapple (f)	(d)		(d)	
Plums (f)	Stew Mix (d)		Eggs (d)	
Prunes (d)	Tomato Cry-		Ice Cream (f)	
Strawberries	stals (d)		Milk (d)	
(f)	Yams (d)		Shortening,	
			powdered (d)	

d: dehydrated; f: freeze-dried.

Barbara G. Salsbury, Just in Case: A Manual of Home Preparedness, Bookcraft Inc.: Salt Lake City, 1975. By permission.

Dehydrated and Freeze-Dried Foods

A wide variety of commercially prepared dehydrated and freeze-dried foods are available for both emergency and long-term storage (see Table 18-6). Both types are either vacuum-packed or packed in an inert gas to restrict the growth of spoilage organisms that require oxygen to grow.

These foods are relatively expensive, but there are advantages: (1) they have an extremely long shelf life and occupy less storage space; (2) because the food is precooked, it is possible to save fuel when using them; (3) there is good retention of natural flavors, coloring, and nutrients; (4) there is no waste; and (5) they are quick and easy to prepare. Freeze-drying also makes possible the long-term storage of real meat and poultry.

Home Canning Techniques

The three home-canning methods are open kettle, water bath, and steam pressure. Correctly applied, each will kill the spoilage organisms naturally present in soil, air, water, and fresh foods.

TABLE 18-7. COST OF HOME FOOD PRESERVATION

| Method | Time | Energy | | Dollar Cost from Kitchen to Table | Quality Satisfaction |
		Fuel	Human Effort		
Freezing	Minimal low	High	Low	Very high	Very high
Canning	Moderate	Moderate	High	Moderate	Moderate to high
Drying	High	Moderate to high	Moderate	Moderate to high	High (specialty items) Low, if only method available
Pickling	High	Low	Moderate	*Depends upon type chosen	High
Storage (Unpro- cessed)	Low to moderate	Low	Moderate (Checking/ culling)	Low	Moderate to high

*Some (such as quick dill pickles) are quick to make, take little effort, and use inexpensive ingredients. Others require prolonged brining over several days' time plus expensive sugar and other ingredients.

U.S. Dept. of Agriculture

OPEN-KETTLE CANNING

This method is used for making jelly. It *must not* be used for fruits, fruit juices, vegetables, or meats because it does not adequately sterilize these foods, and spoilage may result.

WATER-BATH CANNING

Also known as the boiling-water method, this procedure calls for a pot with a rack and lid. This method can be used to process foods that have a high acid content, such as fruits, tomatoes, and pickles. Foods may be packed raw (a water-bath method known as cold or raw pack), or they may be heated or partially cooked first (hot pack). The cold-pack method is simplest and is especially good for small fruits.

The procedure is to place the rack and then hot water in the canner. Fill clean, hot, safety-tempered mason jars with the food and add boiling liquid or syrup. Run a table knife between the food and jar to release air bubbles, and wipe the top and threads of the jars with a clean, damp cloth. Cap the jars, following the jar manufacturer's directions to obtain a proper seal; then stand them on the rack in the canner.

Fill the canner until the jars are covered with one or two inches of water. Be sure to allow two to four inches of space between the top of the jars and the top edge of the canner—so that the water won't boil over. The water should simmer gently or boil briskly, depending on the product. After the recommended time (10 to 30 minutes or longer), remove the jars and allow them to cool for about 12 hours. If using two-piece lids, test each jar to see whether it is properly sealed by tapping the center with a teaspoon for a clear ringing sound. Or press the center; if it doesn't move, the jar is sealed. Remove the band from two-piece lids about a day after canning. Label each jar with the date and contents and store the jars in a cool, dry, dark area.

Never use the water bath method to preserve meat, fish, or poultry or vegetables other than tomatoes.

STEAM-PRESSURE CANNING

This is the only safe way to can meat, poultry, fish, beans, beets, carrots, corns, peppers, and other vegetables. The pressure cooker should be made of heavy aluminum and should have a rack or racks and a cover that locks the vessel tight. The lid has a safety valve, petcock, or vent pipe and a pressure gauge.

Pack the jars the same as for water-bath processing, then put two to three inches of hot water in the cooker and place the jars on the rack. Fasten the cover according to the manufacturer's instructions, and leave the vent open for about 10 minutes or until a steady flow of steam escapes. Cover the petcock or vent valve and bring up the pressure. Process the food for the recommended length of time, following the manufacturer's directions.

Other important advice includes the following:

- Don't experiment or take shortcuts in home canning.
- Use only jars and lids made especially for home canning. Do not use jars with cracks, nicks, or chips.
- Get new rubber rings if you are using one-piece lids, and use new self-seal metal lids if using two-piece lids.
- Don't use overripe food.
- Don't overpack jars.
- Follow exactly the time and temperature specifications for the food and container size. Adjust to your altitude the processing time for water bath and the pressure for steam cookers.

- Don't use canned foods that show signs of spoilage. Watch for bulging lids, leaks, off-odors, or mold. If in doubt, don't even taste the food.
- Boil home-canned vegetables covered for at least 10 minutes before serving. Spoilage signs and odors are more evident in boiling food.
- If the right equipment and supplies are not available for proper canning, it's better not to can.

FINDING FOOD IN NATURE

Flooding or other natural disasters sometimes destroy food supplies along with other property and leave people to their own resources for extended periods. Accidents also leave people stranded in wilderness areas. If such a calamity happened to you, could you handle it? Could you find food, water, and shelter? Or would you "die among plenty," as the saying goes?

Food is relatively plentiful in nature in all but the most extreme instances—if you know how to find it. There are at least 300,000 different kinds of wild plants in the world, and a large number of them are potentially edible, although some are certainly more palatable than others. And there are animals: almost anything that creeps, crawls, swims, or flies is food. Under survival conditions, the kinds of wild plant and animal food available might require that you alter your diet almost completely. But you can survive, and even thrive: wild foods are by and large good foods, with high vitamin and mineral content. The following information should help you understand more about finding food in nature.

Animal Food

Animal food will give you the most food value per pound. With a few exceptions, all animals are edible when freshly killed—even grasshoppers, hairless caterpillars, wood-boring beetle larvae and pupae, ant eggs, and termites. Such insects are high in fat, and you probably have already eaten some of them as contaminants in flour, corn meal, rice, beans, fruits, and various greens that you eat daily.

You should be able to find something to eat wherever you are. One of the best hunting grounds for survival food is along sea coasts, between high- and low-water marks. Other likely spots are the areas between beaches and coral reefs; marshes, mud flats, or mangrove swamps where a river flows into the ocean or into a larger river; river banks, inland waterholes, shores of ponds and lakes; margins of forests, natural meadows, protected mountain slopes, and abandoned cultivated fields. Poorest hunting grounds are high mountain tops, dry ridges, and dense, continuous forest stand.

Hunting Hints

Most warm-blooded, hairy animals are wary and hard to catch. To hunt them requires skill and patience. The best method for a beginner is "still hunting." Find a place where animals pass by frequently—a trail, watering place, or feeding ground. Hide nearby, always downwind so that animals can't smell you, and wait for game to come within range. Remain absolutely motionless. If you have no gun, try to kill animals with a club or sharpened stick used as a spear. You can make a simple slingshot from strips of rubber inner tube and a forked stick. With practice, you can kill any small animal.

You can stalk an animal that is upwind by moving very slowly and noiselessly, keeping under cover as much as possible. Move only when the animal is feeding or looking the other way. Freeze when it looks your way.

The best time to hunt is either in the very early morning or at dusk. In your travels, keep alert for animal signs such as tracks, trampled underbrush, or droppings. On narrow trails, be ready for game using the same pathways.

Game is most plentiful and easiest found near water, in forest clearings, or along the edges of thickets. Many animals live in holes in the ground or in hollow trees. Poke a flexible stick into the hole to determine if it is inhabited. Use a stick to tease the animal into running out, but first close off other exits. Animals in hollow trees can be smoked out by a fire built at the base of the tree; be ready to club the animal as it comes out.

Night hunting or fishing is always good, since most animals move at night. Use a flashlight or make a torch to shine in the animals' eyes. They will be partly blinded by the light, and you can get much closer than in the daytime. Eyes of spiders and insects are good reflectors, so don't be surprised if you "shine up" eyes and can't find the rest of the creature.

Remember that large animals, when wounded or with their young, can be dangerous. Be sure that the animal is dead before getting too close.

Along river and lake shores, small freshwater turtles can often be found sunning themselves. If they dash into shallow water, you can still get them. Watch out for mouth and claws, however.

Frogs and snakes also sun and feed along streams. Use both hands to catch a frog—one to attract it and keep it busy while you grab it with the other. All snakes, except sea snakes, are good to eat; use a long forked stick to catch them. Don't eat toads.

Both marine and dry-land lizards are edible. Use a baited noose or a fine fish hook baited with a bright cloth lure; or use a sling-shot or club.

Don't overlook small birds and their nests. All bird eggs are edible when fresh, even with embryos. Large wading birds, such as cranes and herons, often nest in rookeries or in high trees near water. During the molting season ducks, geese, and swans can be clubbed. Sea birds along low coastlines frequently nest on sand bars or low sand islands. Steep, rocky coasts are favorite rookeries for gulls, auks, and cormorants. Catch birds at night when they are roosting.

Snares, Traps, and Deadfalls

Snaring small game is especially useful in the absence of fire-arms. All snares and traps should be simple in construction and should be made after camp is set up but before darkness. Any spot used as a butchering place attracts other animals; it is a good place to watch for game during the next 24 hours. Use en-trails for bait.

Set your snares in game trails or frequently used runways, which you can recognize by fresh tracks and droppings. Place your traps where the trail is narrow. Arrange pickets, brush, or other obstacles in such a manner as to force the animal to pass through the snare. Be sure the loop is large enough for the head to pass through but not so large that the body will go through. Disturb natural surroundings as little as possible.

Small rodents may be snared with a string noose laid around a hole or burrow. Conceal yourself or lie flat on the ground a short distance away. Jerk the noose tight when the animal pops his head out or steps into the noose.

The twitch-up snare—a noose attached to a sapling—jerks the animal up into the air, kills it promptly, and keeps the carcass out

Figure 18-1. Small-game trail snare with drag. *U.S. Air Force.*

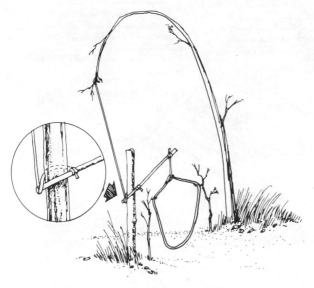

Figure 18-2. Small-animal "twitch-up." *U.S. Air Force.*

of reach of other animals. This type of snare is not recommended for very cold climates, since the bent sapling may freeze in position and will not spring up when released.

Medium to large animals can be captured in dead falls, but this type of trap is recommended only when big game exist in such quantities as to justify the time and effort spent in construction.

Figure 18-3. Hanging snare. *U.S. Air Force.*

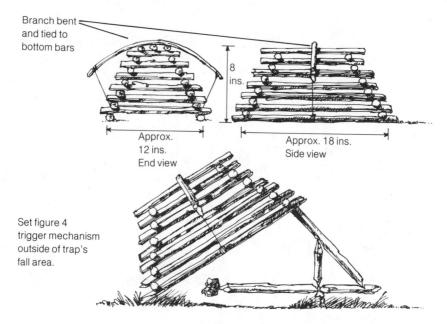

Branch bent and tied to bottom bars

8 ins.

Approx. 12 ins. End view

Approx. 18 ins. Side view

Set figure 4 trigger mechanism outside of trap's fall area.

Figure 18-4. Small-animal trap. *U.S. Air Force.*

Build your deadfall close to a game trail, beside a stream, or on a ridge. Take care to see that the fall log slides smoothly between the upright guide posts and that the bait is placed at a sufficient distance from the bottom log to ensure time for the fall log to drop before the animal can withdraw its head. In a trip-string deadfall, no bait is used. The log is tripped by the animal touching a trip string set across the trail.

162

An untended noose or deadfall is preferred, since it leaves you free for other duties. Check traps early in the morning and late in the afternoon.

Fishing Hints

A simple way to catch fish is with hook and line. Use insects, shellfish, worms, or meat for bait. Try to find out what the fish are eating. Artificial lures can be made from pieces of brightly colored cloth, feathers, or bits of bright metal. A length of wire between the line and the hook will prevent a fish from biting the line in two. If you have no hooks, improvise them from wire or carve them out of bone or hard wood. If the wish won't take bait, try to hook them in the stomach as they swim by. Sometimes you can spear them with a sharpened stick.

Better and more efficient than a line or spear is a net. If you have a seine, attach poles at each end and work it up or down a stream as rapidly as possible, moving stones and thrashing the bottom or the edges of stream banks. Gather up the net quickly every few moments so that the fish will not escape. If you have a gill net, use it in the absolutely quiet water of lakes or streams; stones may be used as anchors and wood for floats. Set the gill net at right angles to shore. You will occasionally catch diving birds trying to rob your gill net.

In fresh water, the deepest water is usually the best place to fish. In shallow streams the best places are pools below falls, at the foot of rapids, or behind rocks. The best time to fish is usually early morning or late evening. Sometimes fishing is best at night, especially if you have a light to attract the fish. Before you give up, try fishing in all kinds of water and depths, at all different times, and with all types of bait.

Fish traps or weirs are very useful for catching both freshwater and saltwater fish, especially those that move in schools. A fish trap is basically an enclosure with a blind opening where two fencelike walls extend out, like a funnel, from the entrance. In lakes or large streams, fish tend to approach the banks and shallows in the morning and evening; sea fish, traveling in large schools, regularly approach the shore with the incoming tide, often moving parallel to the shore and guided by obstructions in the water. A fish trap that intercepts these normal routes of travel can be a very reliable source of food.

163

The time and effort you put into building a fish trap should depend on your need for food and the length of time you plan to stay in one spot. One or two hours of work should do the job if you pick a good location and try to adapt natural features that will reduce your labors. On rocky shores, use natural rock pools. On sandy shores, use sand bars and the ditches they enclose.

Build your simple weir as a low stone wall extending out into the water and forming an angle with the shore. If you plan a more complex brush weir, choose a protected bay or inlet, using the narrowest area and extending one arm almost to the shore, where your trap enclosure waits.

In small, shallow streams, make your fish traps with stakes or brush set into the stream bottom or weighted down with stones so that the stream is almost blocked except for a small, narrow opening into a stone or brush pen of shallow water. Wade into the stream, herding the fish into your trap. Catch or club them when they get into shallow water. Mud-bottomed streams can be trampled until roiled, then seined. The fish are blinded and cannot avoid the nets.

Fish may be confined in properly built enclosures and kept for days, because incoming water keeps them fed. It may be advantageous to keep them alive until needed, thus assuring a fresh supply without danger of spoilage.

Look for fresh water crawfish, snails, and clams under rocks, logs, and overhanging bushes and in mud bottoms.

Mangrove swamps are often good fishing grounds. At low tide, clusters of oysters are exposed, along with mussels, on the mangrove "knees" or lower branches. Clams can be found in mud at the base of trees. Crabs are very active among branches or roots and over mud. Fish can be caught at high tide. Snails are found on mud or clinging to roots. Do not eat shellfish that are not covered at high tide or those from a colony containing obviously diseased members.

Cleaning Fish and Shell Food

Immediately after you land a fish, bleed it by cutting out the gills and the large blood vessels that lie next to the backbone. Scale, eviscerate, and wash the fish in clean water. Some fish (e.g., trout) do not have to be scaled. Others (e.g., catfish and sturgeon) have no scales but can be skinned.

Some small saltwater fish can be eaten with a minimum of cleaning. Their scales are loose and dropped off or can be washed off immediately after they are caught; the stomach and intestines can be flipped out with the thumb. These fish are oily, highly nutritious, and good—even raw.

Clams, oysters, mussels, crabs, and lobsters left in clean water overnight will flush themselves out and save you the work.

Never risk your life with questionable sea food. Never eat fish with slimy gills, sunken eyes, flabby flesh or skin, or an unpleasant odor. If the flesh remains dented after you have pressed your thumb against it, the fish is probably stale.

Getting the Most from Your Game

In a survival situation, you must be prepared to take full advantage of a game carcass. Many people have died from starvation because they used only part of a carcass and abandoned the rest on the mistaken theory that they could secure more game whenever needed. It simply isn't that easy. Under survival conditions, therefore, skinning and butchering must be done so that every edible pound of meat is saved.

To avoid spoilage, eat the heart, liver, and kidneys as soon as possible. All the meaty parts of the skull, including the brain, tongue, eyes, and flesh, can also be eaten. In a severe hunger emergency, the intestines are palatable if thoroughly cleaned in water, then wrapped around a stick and roasted over coals. The large intestine, cooked in this manner, is considered by some a delicacy.

Take care not to discard edible fat. Fat must be eaten in order to provide a complete diet. Many people think they are unable to eat fat, probably because it's not a necessity in a plentiful, civilized diet. Under emergency conditions, however, when sugar or vegetable oils may be lacking, fat *must* be eaten. Rabbits lack fat; and the fact that a person can die on a diet of rabbit meat alone indicates the importance of fat in a primitive diet.

Transporting Game Animals

A procedure often advocated for transporting a kill is to use the skin as a sled for dragging the meat to camp. For a large animal, this procedure may prove satisfactory only on frozen lakes or rivers, or over very smooth, snow-covered terrain. In rough or bush-covered country, it is generally most difficult, if not impossible.

However, large animals frequently can be dragged down a snow-filled gully to the base of a mountain. If meat is the only consideration, and you do not care about the condition of the skin, mountain game can sometimes be rolled for long distances. First, gut the animal and sew up the incision. Once you reach the bottom of the hill, almost invariably the method is to backpack your meat, making several trips if there is no one else to help.

When the weight of the animal proves excessive, eat some of the meat at the scene of the kill. Also remove the bones from the meat. Leg bones laid on a bed of coals roast quickly and can easily be cracked with light taps of a knife or stone to expose the marrow, a food highly prized by many hunters.

The greatest danger to meat comes during weather warm enough to allow flies to deposit their eggs, or "blow" the meat. Even while you are cleaning or skinning an animal, flies can enter bullet holes or any small cavity and lay eggs, which turn into maggots in a few days. The *only* way to prevent fly-blow is to make it impossible for a fly to touch the meat. Do this by wrapping the meat in cloth. Wrap it loosely, so that an airspace of an inch or two is formed between the meat and the sack.

When meat is to be backpacked during the day, it should be rolled in fabric or clothing and placed inside the pack to be carried. This soft material keeps the meat clean and acts as a nonconductor, keeping the meat cool.

Skinning and Butchering

Immediately after a kill is the best time to skin and butcher. However, if you kill an animal late in the day, you can simply gut the animal and return early the next morning to do the skinning. Be sure to place the carcass out of reach of predators; this way, if the site is visited, the marauder usually will eat only the entrails.

The first step in skinning is to turn the animal on its back and, with a sharp knife, cut through the skin on a straight line from the end of the tail bone to a point under its neck (A–C on Figure 18-5). In making this cut, pass around the anus and, with great care, press the skin open until you can insert the first two fingers between the skin and the thin membrane enclosing the viscera. When the fingers can be forced forward, place the blade of the knife between the fingers, blade up, with the knife held firmly. As you force the fingers forward, palm upward, follow the knife blade, cutting the skin but not the membrane.

166

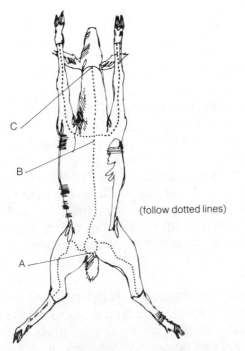

C

B

(follow dotted lines)

A

Figure 18-5. Where to make preliminary cuts. *U.S. Air Force.*

If the animal is male, cut the skin parallel to, but not touching, the penis. If the tube leading from the bladder is accidently cut, a messy job and unclean meat will result. If the gall or urine bladders are broken, washing will help clean the meat. Otherwise, it is best not to wash the meat but to allow it to form a protective glaze.

On reaching the ribs, it is no longer possible to force fingers forward, because the skin adheres more strongly to flesh and bone. Furthermore, care is no longer necessary because you won't be cutting into viscera. The cut to point C can be quickly completed by alternately forcing the knife under the skin and lifting it. With the central cut completed, make side cuts consisting of incisions through the skin, running from central cut A–C up the inside of each leg to the knee and hock joints. Then make cuts around the front legs just above the knee and around the hind legs above the hocks. Make the final cross cut at point C, and then cut completely around the neck and the back of the ears. Now is the time to begin skinning.

On a small or medium-sized animal, one person can skin on each side. The easiest method is to begin at the corners where the cuts meet. When the animal is large, three people can skin at the same time. However, you should remember that when it is getting dark and hands are clumsy because of the cold, a sharp skinning knife can make a deep wound. So keep well away from the person next to you.

When you have skinned down on the animal's side as far as you can, roll the carcass on its side to continue on the back. Before doing so, spread out the loose skin to prevent the meat from touching the ground and picking up sand and dirt. Follow the same procedure on the opposite side until the skin is free.

In opening the membrane that encloses the viscera, follow the same procedure you followed in cutting the skin by using the fingers of one hand as a guard for the knife and to separate the intestines from the membrane. You can cut away this thin membrane along the ribs and sides in order to see better. Be careful not to cut the intestines or bladder. The large intestine passes through an aperture in the pelvis. This tube must be separated with a knife from the bone surrounding it. Tie a knot in the bladder tube to prevent the escape of urine. With these steps accomplished, the insides can be easily disengaged from the back and removed from the carcass.

The intestines of a well-conditioned animal are covered with a lacelike layer of fat, which can be lifted off and placed on nearby bushes to dry for later use. The kidneys are embedded in the back, forward of the pelvis, and are covered with fat. Running forward from the kidneys on each side of the backbone are two long strips of chop meat or muscle called tenderloin or backstrap. Eat this after the liver, heart, and kidneys, because it usually is very tender. Edible meat can also be removed from the head, brisket, ribs, backbone, and pelvis.

Large animals should be quartered. To do this, cut down between the first and second ribs and then sever the backbone with an axe. Cut through the brisket of the front half and then chop lengthwise through the backbone so that you have two front quarters. On the rear half, cut through the pelvic bone and lengthwise through the backbone. When speed is advisable, the front legs and shoulders can be quickly separated from the body with a knife.

Avoid cutting into or squeezing musk glands. Deer have musk glands on their hind legs, at the hock joints. If necessary to remove them, use great care.

168

Badgers, skunks, mink, and otter have anal glands; be very careful with them. Most of the objectionable odor of small rodents is removed by skinning.

Birds should be handled in the same manner as other animals. They should be gutted after killing and protected from flies. Birds that carry no fat, such as ptarmigan, crow, and owl, may be skinned. The skins of waterfowl are usually fat, and for this reason these birds should be plucked and cooked with the skin on. The giblets may also be eaten. The flesh of carrion-eating birds, such as vultures, is unpleasant to the taste; it must be boiled for at least 20 minutes, to kill parasites, before further cooking or eating. Fish-eating birds have a strong, fish-oil flavor. This may be lessened by baking them in mud or by skinning them before cooking.

The best meat on a lizard is the hind quarters and tail. Eat the legs of a frog. Turtles have edible flesh on the legs, neck, and tail and on other parts of the body. Skin all frogs and snakes, and remove the head and viscera.

Cooking

Cooking, of course, makes for a more enjoyable meal. Hawks and crows, for example, can be tough, but they soften up when stewed; and plant foods are made more digestible and palatable, and they yield more food value, after heating. But for safety's sake, as well, all wild game, freshwater fish, clams, mussels, snails, and crayfish must be thoroughly cooked. Raw or smoked freshwater fish are frequently contaminated with tapeworm and lung fluke parasites which are destroyed by thorough cooking. Saltwater shellfish may be eaten raw but are safest when cooked.

Shark meat is edible except in the arctic, but it must first be cut into small pieces and soaked overnight or boiled in several changes of water to get rid of the ammonia flavor which accumulates in the flesh. Shark meat is not poisonous, just unpalatable.

Turtle eggs can be boiled or roasted, but the whites will not harden.

Boiling, roasting, baking, and frying—in that order of preference—are efficient ways of preparing foods. Pit cooking and clambake-style cooking are slower but require less attention and they protect food from flies and other pests.

ROASTING IN THE COALS OF A FIRE

You can coat fish, potatoes, and many other large foods with a layer of mud or clay and roast them directly in the flames or coals of a fire. Loss of food by burning is thus reduced. You need not scale fish prepared in this way; when the fish is cooked, the skin peels off with the baked clay.

STEAMING UNDER THE FIRE

Foods small in size, such as small bird eggs, freshwater snails, and shellfish, may be cooked in quantity in a pit beneath your fire. Fill a small, shallow pit with food, after lining it or wrapping the food in plant leaves or cloth. Cover the pit with a ¼- to ½-inch layer of sand or soil, and build your fire directly over it. After sufficient cooking (one hour), rake away the fire and remove the food.

STEAMING WITH HEATED STONES (CLAMBAKE STYLE)

Heat a number of stones in a fire, then allow the fire to burn down to coals. Place such foods as freshwater mussels (in their shells) directly on and between the stones, and cover the whole with plant leaves, grass, or seaweed, and also with a layer of sand or soil. When thoroughly steamed in their own juices, clams, oysters, and mussels will show a gaping shell when uncovered; you may eat the food without further preparation.

STONE BOILING

Fill a big container with water and food. Add hot stones until the water boils. Cover with big leaves for about an hour, or until food is well done.

SOLAR OVEN

A recent outgrowth of the increased concern for energy conservation is the solar oven. Instructions for building solar ovens are available in numerous publications.

Preserving Excess Food

Cutting meat across the grain in thin strips and either drying it in the hot sun or smoking it over a slow fire will produce "jerky." In warm or damp weather, when meat deteriorates rapidly, smoking can keep it from spoiling for some time.

Efficient smoking can be accomplished by laying fabric over a drying rack and building the fire underneath. Lay the thin strips of meat on the rack. Take care to keep the meat from getting too hot. Willow, alder, cottonwood, birch, and dwarf birch make the best smoking woods. Do not use pitch woods, such as fir and pine: they make the meat unpalatable.

Hang all drying meat high to keep it away from animals, and cover it to prevent blowfly infestation. If mold forms on the outside, brush or wash it off before you eat the meat. In damp weather, smoke or air-dried meat must be redried to prevent mold.

Reptile meat may be dried by placing it on hot rocks or hanging it in the sun.

Fish can be split (cut off the head and remove the backbone), spread apart, and cut thin. Then dry it over smoke fires, spread it on hot rocks, or hang it from branches in the sun. If sea water is available, splash it on the fish from time to time to salt the outside. Do not keep any seafood unless it is well dried and salted.

To preserve cooked animal food, recook it once each day, especially in warm weather.

Plant Foods

Plants are more common than animals, so use them all you can. You should, however, have some practical knowledge of wild edible and poisonous plants, where they grow, and how to use them. Very few are deadly when eaten in small quantities (see edibility rules below). On the contrary, your greatest enemies under survival conditions are the decay bacteria that may infect your food under makeshift sanitary conditions.

Complete descriptions of all wild food plants are beyond the scope of this work; therefore, the information here is limited to a general discussion of classes of food plants, with illustrations of several representative types.

The best way to familiarize yourself with the appearance of edible plants is to have someone point them out to you. Each time you are shown a plant, make a mental note of the kind of place (habitat) in which you find it. Without any particular effort, you will soon find that you are learning many kinds of plants at sight: palms, breadfruit, and plantains in the tropics; beans, succulent bushes, and water-indicating plants in the desert; blueberries, crowberries, and wild rhubarb in the cold regions.

You must use intelligence in coping with your survival problems. Learn to recognize vegetation *patterns* in the tropics, deserts, and cold zones. The fact that you have learned about palms, beans, and wild rhubarb in one locality may pay you dividends if you are forced to survive in similar remote places.

171

Edibility Rules

As a general rule, poisonous plants are not a serious hazard, except on those rare occasions when you may accidently walk into a patch of them. Your chances of eating a poisonous plant are small. Frequently, only seeds are poisonous, but use care in selecting any plant part. Use these rules as a guide:

- Cook all plant foods when in doubt about their edibility. Some poisons may be removed by cooking.
- Never eat large quantities of a strange plant food without first testing it. A small quantity of even poisonous food is not likely to prove fatal or even dangerous, whereas a large quantity may be. (This does not apply to mushrooms, which are best avoided in any case.) Take a teaspoonful of the plant food, prepared in the way it will be used (raw, boiled, baked, etc.), and hold it in your mouth for about 5 minutes. If, by this time, no burning sensation or other unpleasant effect has occurred, swallow it. Wait 8 hours. If no ill effects such as nausea, cramps, or diarrhea come about, eat a handful and wait another 8 hours. If no ill effects show up at the end of this time, the plant may be considered edible. Keep in mind, however, that any new or strange food should be eaten with restraint until you have become accustomed to it.
- Avoid eating plants that have a disagreeable taste (bitterness is a guide) or an unpleasant odor. Remember, however, that olives are bitter and grapefruit is sour, so an unpleasant taste does not, in itself, necessarily mean poison. But a burning, nauseating, or very bitter taste is a warning of danger. A disagreeable taste in food otherwise safe to eat can sometimes be removed by leaching—that is, pouring cold or hot water through the chopped, crushed, or ground material. If cooking is possible, boiling in one or more changes of water may remove the unpleasant taste.
- Poisonous mushrooms and other poisonous fungi cannot be detected by disagreeable taste or unpleasant odor. Some mushrooms and other fungi are edible; however, they would normally contribute little enough food value and are easily enough confused with poisonous types that they should be disregarded as a food source unless you are thoroughly familiar with them.
- Avoid eating untested plants with milky juice, and avoid letting the milk contact your skin (except for the numerous kinds of

172

wild fig, breadfruit, and papaya, which are safe despite the milky juice).

- To avoid ergot poisoning from infected heads of cereals or grasses, discard all grain heads having black spurs in place of normal seed grains.

- In general, it is safe to try foods that you observe being eaten by birds and mammals, although there are some exceptions. Food eaten by rodents (mice, rats, rabbits, beavers, squirrels, muskrats) or by bears, raccoons, and various other omnivorous animals are usually safe to for you to try.

- Beware of contact poisons. The relatively few plants that act as skin irritants all belong to the same natural family of plants as poison ivy, poison sumac, and poison oak (cashew family). The plants of this family are trees or shrubs, usually with a resinous bark. The leaves are usually alternate on the stem and divided into three segments, or pinnate like the ribs of a feather. The fruit is usually one-seeded with an outer fleshy covering—similar to a cherry. Some of these plants exude black ooze from fresh wounds. The poison ingredient is the same, and the treatment is identical to that for persons coming into contact with poison ivy.

Selecting Edible Plants

A large number of plants, whether water or land types in arctic, desert, or tropical regions, furnish edible fruits, seeds, bark, tubers, buds, leaves, flowers, sap, pods, nuts, stems, shoots, rootstalks, or bulbs. All of some plants are edible, but for most kinds it is necessary to select the most palatable part, whether it be root or fruit, leaves or pods. Perhaps only the nuts will be edible. Flesh-leafed plants often make good salad greens, and fresh fruits provide fluid when water supplies are low.

Ordinarily, water used to boil plant roots, tubers, or seeds becomes a good broth with the addition of seafood or meat. To give taste to stews, add wild onions, succulent stems, and leaves of plants.

Most plant foods can be dried by wind, sun, or fire with or without smoke—or a combination of these can be used.

STARCHY FOODS

Many plants store large quantities of edible starch, in underground parts and in stalks, stems, and seeds. All starchy foods must be cooked: raw starch is difficult to digest.

Tubers of the wild potato (mostly tropical American) are edible if the plant has foliage similar to that of the domesticated potato. The tubers of other plants, such as the tropical yam and water lily, are abundant in the tropics. All these can be boiled, but they are more easily baked or roasted.

Rootstalks are found in thousands of widely distributed plants, among them ferns and cattail.

Bulbs are produced most commonly by members of the lily family, such as the true lily, onion, tulip, and daffodil. Many kinds of bulbs are edible.

Tubers, rootstalks, and bulbs are usually available throughout the year in most regions. In cold climates, these underground storage organs can be found by digging where the dried plant stalks remain.

Stems of the sego palm, cycad, and certain other palms produce large quantities of edible starch in the trunk—enough to sustain life for several weeks.

Grasses are a very important source of survival food, especially in warmer parts of the world. Wild grasses, in general, have an abundance of seeds, which may be eaten boiled or roasted after you have separated the chaff from the seeds by rubbing. Grains or seeds of millet, wild grasses, wild rye, and many other grasses are starchy and serve as excellent staple food.

No known grass is poisonous. If the kernels are still soft and do not have large, stiff barbs attached, you may boil them for porridge. To gather grass seeds, place a cloth on the ground and beat the grass heads with sticks (winnowing). Many grasses pop like popcorn. Try them out by heating them in a closed vessel.

Fruits of the green banana (table variety), the plantain (cooking banana), and the breadfruit, all tropical, contain plenty of starch. Succulent fruits are best boiled. Large, tough, or heavy-skinned fruits are best baked or roasted.

VEGETABLES

Vegetables are produced mostly from succulent leaves, pods, seeds, stems, and nonwoody roots. Select young, tender kinds, but cook all vegetables. Cooking will normally destroy all injurious intestinal parasites or bacteria.

Many ferns are edible; none are poisonous. Edible kinds occur mainly in forested areas in the warm temperate and tropical regions. Some are only a few inches high; on the other hand, tree ferns up to 100 feet tall are found in tropical areas from sea level to mountain slopes, wherever there is heavy rainfall. Desert ferns usually are small and tough. In the far North, ferns are few and very small; look for edible varieties in moist, shady places.

Eat the fiddleheads of ferns. These are the curled, young, succulent fronds which are as good as cabbage or asparagus in food value. Practically all fiddleheads are covered with "hair" that makes them bitter; remove it by rubbing them in water before preparing them for eating. If the fiddleheads are especially bitter, boil them for 10 minutes, then reboil them in fresh water for 30 to 40 minutes. Bird eggs or meat may be cooked with the fiddleheads.

NUTS

Edible nuts are the most sustaining of all raw forest foods and are found throughout the world. Many American nut trees, such as oaks, hickories, hazelnuts, and beechnuts, are widely distributed throughout the north temperate zone. Others, such as the coconut and cashew, occur widely in the tropics. Several kinds of evergreen trees, especially pines, produce edible seeds that you can get by shaking or breaking open the cones. Familiarity with some of the common North American nut trees will help you locate nut-bearing trees in other regions.

Most nuts can be eaten raw, but some, such as acorns, are better cooked. Acorns should be broken up, boiled with ashes from the fire to eliminate tannin, molded into cakes, and then baked.

BARK

You may eat the inner bark from numerous trees either raw or cooked. In famine areas, people make flour from the inner bark of trees. The thin, green, outer bark and the white, innermost bark are normally used for food. Brown bark ordinarily contains a great deal of tannin.

Among trees with bark that is used as a source of food are the poplars (including cottonwoods and aspens), birches, and willows. The inner bark and growing tips of a few species of pine can also be used. Pine bark is especially valuable for vitamin C. The outer bark of these pines is scraped away and the inner bark stripped from the trunk and eaten fresh, dried, or cooked. It may also be pulverized into flour.

Bark is most palatable when newly formed in the spring. As food, it can be very useful in arctic regions, where resources may be scarce, especially in winter. The needles of evergreens may be boiled as tea.

WATER PLANTS

Plants that grow in very wet places along margins of rivers, lakes, and ponds, and those growing directly in water are of potential value as survival food. The succulent underground parts and stems are what is most frequently eaten. Poisonous water plants are rare. In temperate climates the water hemlock is the most poisonous plant to be found around marshes and ponds.

The cattail is found worldwide, except in the tundra regions of the far North. Expect to find cattails in the more moist places of desert areas in all continents as well as the moist tropics and temperate zones of both hemispheres. Eat the young shoots, which taste like asparagus. The rootstalks, without the outer covering, are eaten boiled or raw. While the plant is in flower, the yellow pollen is very abundant; this may be mixed with water into small cakes and steamed as a kind of bread.

Water lilies occur in all the continents but principally in southern Asia, Africa, and North and South America. Two main types occur: (1) temperate water lilies, which produce enormous rootstalks and yellow or white flowers that float on the water surface; and (2) tropical water lilies, which produce large, edible tubers and flowers that are elevated above the water surface. Rootstalks or tubers may be difficult to obtain in deep water, but they are starchy and therefore full of food if you can reach them. Eat them raw or boiled. Stems may be cooked in a stew. Young seed pods may be sliced and eaten as a vegetable. Seeds may be bitter, but they are very nourishing. When parched, they may be rubbed between stones to produce flour. People in many parts of the world consider the water lily an important food item.

Many seaweeds are edible, but never eat them in quantity; most are violent purgatives, although none is actually poisonous. They may certainly be eaten in small amounts as flavoring in other foods. All seaweeds are rich in iodine, minerals, and vitamins. They will prevent scurvy. Some have too much lime carbonate or are too horny to be eaten. Others are covered with slime.

In selecting seaweed for food, choose only plants attached to rocks or floating free. Do not take plants stranded on the beach. A coarse, dark green seaweed with large air bladders is rockweed. It does not have food value, but in and under it you will find small crabs, shrimp, and shellfish.

To prepare seaweed for food, wash it in water, dry it in the sun on a wood or stone platform, pulverize it by pounding, and sprinkle it over other food.

GROWING VEGETABLES FOR LONG-TERM SURVIVAL

Growing a home garden can be a satisfying activity, and a productive one as well. The vegetables it produces can save your family hundreds of dollars each year under normal circumstances. During food shortages, and following disasters that do not destroy everything, a garden can be much more: it could be one of the only sources of food at your disposal. It is wise, therefore, to know something of the basics of growing a garden before the need actually arises. The following are some of the important principles to keep in mind.

Selecting a Site

For best results, the ground should be fertile, well drained, and level. The site should have at least six hours of full sunlight or more every day.

Try to put the garden near a source of water. Be aware of trees that may shade the area and whose roots may compete with your vegetables for vital nutrients and water.

Make a plan on paper, showing the required distance between rows and the expected harvest dates.

Determining When to Plant

A common mistake is planting too soon. Find the expected frost-free dates for the area—sometimes temperatures can be five degrees warmer in the city than in suburbs. Planting and harvesting times vary from region to region and differ among vegetables, too. The frost-free date in spring is usually two to three weeks later than the average date of the last freeze in a locality and is approximately the date that oak trees leaf out (if oak trees grow in the area).

For early yields, raising seedlings indoors and transplanting them outdoors when the soil warms up is suggested.

Selecting Seed

Important things to consider when you're trying to decide what and how much to grow are: nutritional values, kinds of fruits and vegetables best liked by the family, the kinds that grow best in your area, and the amount of gardening space available.

Most of the leafy-green and yellow vegetables are among the best sources of vitamins A and C. Some are good sources of other vitamins and minerals, and others provide important bulk in the diet. Table 18-8 should help you decide which vegetables to plant. Choosing two or three from each nutritional group will contribute much to a balanced diet.

Many disease-resistant varieties and strains are now available. It is generally advisable to purchase new seed each year. However, seed for some vegetables can be kept in viable condition several years if it is stored in a cool, dry place (preferably in an airtight container) and protected from rats, mice, and weevils.

Under normal circumstances, it is usually not wise to harvest and save your own seed from the garden. Many splendid hybrid

TABLE 18-8. SOME COMMON VEGETABLES GROUPED ACCORDING TO THE APPROXIMATE TIMES THEY CAN BE PLANTED AND THEIR RELATIVE REQUIREMENTS FOR COOL AND WARM WEATHER

Cold-hardy plants for early-spring planting		Cold-tender or heat-hardy plants for later-spring or early-summer planting				Hardy plants for late-summer or fall planting except in the North (plant 6 to 8 weeks before first fall freeze)
Very hardy (plant 4 to 6 weeks before frost-free date)	Hardy (plant 2 to 4 weeks before frost-free date)	Not cold-hardy (plant on frost-free date)	Requiring hot weather (plant 1 week or more after frost-free date)	Medium heat-tolerant (good for summer planting)		
Broccoli	Beets	Beans, snap	Beans, lima	Beans, all		Beets
Cabbage	Carrot	Okra	Eggplant	Chard		Collard
Lettuce	Chard	New Zealand spinach	Peppers	Soybean		Kale
Onions	Mustard	Soybean	Sweet potato	New Zealand spinach		Lettuce
Peas	Parsnip	Squash	Cucumber	Squash		Mustard
Potato	Radish	Sweet corn	Melons	Sweet corn		Spinach
Spinach		Tomato				Turnip
Turnip						

U.S. Dept. of Agriculture.

plants will either produce no seed at all, or will only produce inferior offspring. However, in some emergency situations you may not have any choice but to use whatever seed you can get wherever you can get it.

Succession Planting

To get the most from a garden, practice succession planting (double cropping). This means getting two crops from each garden row—one that can be harvested in early summer, the other in fall. Often the fall garden is more productive, and fall-grown vegetables are usually of better quality for canning than those that mature during the hot, dry periods of midsummer. There are fast-growing varieties of the following vegetables that can be ready to harvest in about the number of days noted: garden cress, 10 days; radishes, 25 days; mustard greens, 35 days; looseleaf lettuce, 40 days; spinach, 42 days; turnips, 45 days; summer squash, 50 days; snap beans, early peas, and kale, 55 days; Swiss chard, 60 days.

Caring for the Garden

In most areas a garden requires a moisture supply equivalent to about an inch of rain a week during the growing season for best plant growth. It is much better to give the garden a good soaking about once a week than to water it sparingly more often. Light sprinklings at frequent intervals do little, if any, good.

After each rain or watering, the garden should be thoroughly hoed to kill weeds that have sprouted. Mulching vegetable crops with organic materials is a good practice. This can be done by applying mulch about 4 to 6 inches deep when the plants are about 6 inches tall. Before applying mulch, hoe out all small weeds. Not only does mulch control weeds, it also conserves moisture, keeps the soil from packing, and increases the humus necessary for vigorous plant growth.

Clouds may indicate bad weather. *Courtesy Nelson Wadsworth.*

19. WEATHER FORECASTING

Before the advent of radio and television, people had to be their own weather forecasters. They learned how to spot impending weather-related problems by the signs that nature exhibited: specific cloud patterns, changes in wind direction, animal behavior, and so on.

It is not difficult to be your own weather forecaster. In fact, in a major disaster or other emergency situation, you may be forced to predict the weather in order to avoid further difficulties.

Bad-Weather Signs

The following rules of thumb and sayings have served for many years as signs of imminent bad weather. It should be remembered, though, that exceptions occur, and not all of these rules are applicable in every locale. Try them out in your area; if they work, you'll have some valuable and intriguing information for future reference.

- A ring around the sun or moon means rain or snow. (The "ring" is light reflected off very high, thin clouds, which often precede stormy weather.)
- Windshifts from north to west then south are often accompanied by rain. (This applies particularly to Northern Hemisphere areas where storm systems, with winds rotating counterclockwise if viewed from above, follow the normal west-to-east prevailing winds.)
- Unusual sky tints—green, yellow, dark red, or gloomy blue—bring wind or rain or both.
- Small, inky clouds bring rain.
- Clouds hanging on the heights indicate wind and rain unless they lift by midday.
- Scud clouds (small, dark, scurrying cumulus types) sweeping beneath a dark stratus layer mean that wind and rain may be near. If they are above the stratus layer (which may be difficult to see), there will be wind only.

- Cloud layers moving in different directions foretell a change in wind direction to that of the upper layer.
- "Red sky in the morning, sailor take warning.
  Red sky at night, sailor's delight."
- "A red sky has water in his eye."
- "Evening red and morning gray,
  Sets the traveler on his way;
  Evening gray and morning red,
  Brings down rain upon his head."
- "Rain before seven, clear before eleven."
- "When the dew is on the grass,
  Rain will never come to pass."
- "When the stars begin to huddle,
  The earth will soon become a puddle."
- "Clear moon, frost soon."
- "A ring around the moon means rain;
  The larger the ring, the sooner the rain."
- "Sound traveling far and wide
  A stormy day will betide."

Fair Weather Signs

- Wind shifts from south to west then north are often accompanied by clearing.
- Red sky in the evening means fine, generally warm weather for the next day.
- A gray dawn means fine weather.
- The higher the clouds, the finer the weather.
- Cumulus clouds, especially those found on bright, sunny days, mean fair weather unless they tower and flatten on top.
- Fog in the valleys will burn off and clear.
- Rain rarely falls after dew forms.

Estimating Wind Velocity

In 1806, Sir Francis Beaufort, a British Admiral, developed a method for determining wind velocity, a method still used by the U.S. National Weather Service in their weather forecasts. It is shown in the following table:

By helping you become familiar with the various classifications and their characteristics, this table can be a great aid to you in determining the wind-chill factor. (See page 66.)

TABLE 19-1. ESTIMATING WIND VELOCITY FROM SIMPLE OBSERVATIONS

If you See . . .	The Wind Is Probably Blowing . . .
Flags or pennants hanging limp from their staffs; smoke rising vertically from chimneys and open fires	0–1 mph
Flags and pennants barely moving; leaves moving slightly on trees; smoke drifting lazily with the wind	1–3 mph
Flags and pennants moving slightly out from their staffs; leaves rustling in trees; if you feel wind on your face	4–7 mph
Flags and pennants standing out from their staffs at an angle of 30 to 45°; or leaves and twigs in constant motion	8–12 mph
Small branches moving in trees; dust and paper being blown about	13–18 mph
Flags and pennants flying at 90° angle; small trees swaying	19–24 mph
Flags and pennants standing straight out from their staffs and fluttering vigorously; large tree branches in motion; or if you hear whistling in power lines	25–31 mph
Flags and pennants whipping about wildly on the staffs; whole trees in motion; loose objects being picked up and blown about; or if you find it somewhat difficult to walk when facing the wind	32–38 mph
Twigs being broken from trees; drivers having a problem in controlling their vehicles; or if you hear power lines whining loudly	39–46 mph
Trees bending sharply; structural damage occurring in buildings; the progress of vehicles and pedestrians alike being seriously impeded	47–54 mph
Trees being uprooted; considerable structural damage occurring	55–63 mph
Buildings suffering severe damage	63–72 mph
Widespread destruction; or if walking is virtually impossible	more than 72 mph

Figure 20-1. Body signals. *U.S. Air Force.*

Our receiver
operating

Use drop
message

All well

Affirmative
(Yes)

Negative
(No)

Require mechanical
help or parts

Pick us up

Do not land here

Can proceed shortly;
wait if possible

Require medical help
URGENTLY

Land here (pointing in
direction of landing)

20. SIGNALING

Many emergency conditions require a search for people in distress. Under such circumstances, it is always better if those being sought know how to make their presence and their location very conspicuous. One man, or even a large group of people, cannot be spotted easily from the air, especially when visibility is limited. For this reason, many signals have been devised over the years to indicate a condition of distress or other emergency status. Among these are the following:

- The standard "SOS"—a signal consisting of the letters *SOS* in Morse code (a pattern of 3 short, 3 long, 3 short), repeated at intervals. The SOS may be an audible signal, flashes of light, a tone transmitted by radio, etc.
- The word *Mayday* transmitted by radio. "Mayday" is reserved strictly for emergency use, and may be either a voice or code transmission.
- The continuous sounding of a foghorn or any fog-signaling apparatus.
- A dog, police, or referee's whistle successively blown (for example, 6 whistle blasts in one minute, then a minute's silence, then 6 more blasts).
- Three gunshots fired in rapid succession, *or* a gun or other explosive signal continuously fired at intervals of about one minute.
- Smoke signals—either the large volume of orange-colored smoke from a typical signal grenade, or smoke from a signal fire. Three signals fires in a triangle is a positive signal of distress. (Note: Black smoke from burning rubber, etc., is more likely to attract attention than white smoke.)
- Bright signal fires for night rescue.
- Aerial red flares, or red automobile warning flares.
- Flashes from a signal mirror.
- Slowly and repeatedly raising and lowering arms outstretched to each side.

185

- Large letters or other figures tramped in snow or laid out in other terrain for aircraft to see.
- Emergency homing transmitters (many aircraft are equipped with these in case of accident).

In general, use smoke by day and bright flame by night if other signaling devices are not available. Add engine oil, rags soaked in oil, or pieces of rubber to your fire to make black smoke; add green leaves, moss, or a little water to send up billows of white smoke. Keep plenty of spare fuel on hand.

All signaling aids, especially flares, must be kept dry and in good condition.

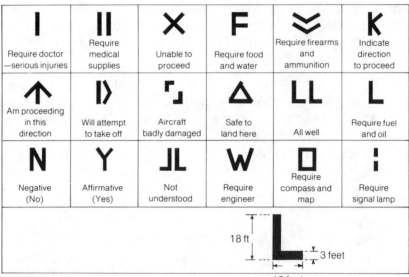

I	**II**	**X**	**F**	**⩘**	**K**
Require doctor —serious injuries	Require medical supplies	Unable to proceed	Require food and water	Require firearms and ammunition	Indicate direction to proceed
↑	**I)**	**⌐」**	**△**	**LL**	**L**
Am proceeding in this direction	Will attempt to take off	Aircraft badly damaged	Safe to land here	All well	Require fuel and oil
N	**Y**	**⅃L**	**W**	**□**	**⋮**
Negative (No)	Affirmative (Yes)	Not understood	Require engineer	Require compass and map	Require signal lamp

18 ft — 3 feet — 12 feet

Figure 20-2. Pattern signals. *U.S. Air Force.*

How to Use a Signal Mirror

A signaling mirror is one of the most effective means of sending a distress message. On hazy days, aircraft can see the flash of a mirror before survivors can see the aircraft; so it is wise to flash the mirror in the direction of a plane when you hear it, even when you cannot see it. Mirror flashes have been spotted by rescue aircraft more than 20 miles away.

To use a signaling mirror, follow this procedure:

1. Reflect sunlight from the mirror onto a nearby surface.

2. Slowly bring the mirror up to eye level and look through the sighting hole. You will see a bright spot of light: this is the aim indicator.

3. Hold the mirror near the eye and slowly turn and manipulate it so that the bright spot of light is on the target.

A mirror can be improvised by punching a hole in the middle of an ordinary mirror's reflecting surface. Practicing signaling with your mirror, and always keep it clean.

If you only have a broken piece of glass or a mirror with no sighting hole, try this:

1. Hold the mirror up to the sun with one hand, and stretch your other hand out in front of you so that it blots out the view of your target.

2. Hit your extended hand with a reflection of the sun from the glass or mirror.

3. Sight your target through the slits between your fingers while you keep the mirror flashing on that hand—then lower the hand. The flash of light will then be aimed at the target.

Figure 20-3. Signal-mirror technique. *U.S. Air Force.*

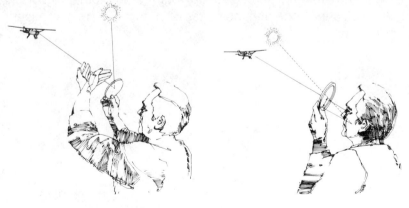

In Cold Weather

If you are among buildings, one way to make your presence more conspicuous is to keep snow and frost off roofs and other surfaces so that the structures make a sharp contrast with the surroundings.

You can also tramp out signals in the snow and fill them with tree boughs, sod, or ashes to make them even more visible. In brushy country, cut conspicuous patterns in vegetation.

If you use a signal fire, build it on a platform so that it will not sink into the snow. Build a "bird nest" of quickly flammable material to ensure a quick start for your signal fire. Remember, too, that *sound does not carry well through snow.* If you take shelter in a house or other structure, you may not hear approaching aircraft. So keep someone on guard as a spotter. Build the spotter a windbreak, but don't roof it.

In Desert Areas

One of the biggest ways to construct a signal in desert areas is to dig trenches or line up rocks so that they will create shadows in the form of letters or other figures.

A mirror is also a very good distress signal; practice using it.

Smoke fires are best for use in daytime; flares and bright flames are easier to see at night. If there is any brush in the area, gather it in piles and have it ready to light.

In the Tropics

In areas of dense tree and brush growth, signals are very difficult to see. Therefore, be sure to set up your fires and other signals in natural clearings or along the edges of streams—or make a clearing yourself.

21. SURVIVAL WEAPONS: RIFLE, AXE, KNIFE

Today the rifle, axe, and knife are not nearly as crucial to everyday existence as they were in pioneering circumstances a century ago. However, in many difficult situations, the need for these important survival tools is keenly felt, and finding suitable substitutes is often extremely difficult.

Firearms

Two separate categories of guns are usually considered for survival: (1) weapons for defense, and (2) firearms to help provide a continuing supply of food.

Weapons for defense are outside the scope of this work; therefore, no recommendation will be made. Moreover, the decision as to whether or not a person will want to use a firearm to protect himself, others, food, and other supplies involves too many unknowns and is perhaps best left to the individual.

However, a survival weapon that will provide food should be seriously considered. When you look for a suitable weapon, consider the type of game animals and terrain in the area you have in mind. The familiar sporting guns are fine for hunting large and small game, and for predator and pest control. Stay with the most popular calibers, since ammunition is easier to obtain under most circumstances. You may even choose to learn how to reload your own ammunition, although acquiring this skill can be quite an undertaking. Spare parts and ease of repair are other considerations when selecting a firearm. All rifles with telescopic sights should also have a set of iron sights, in case the scope gets damaged.

A handgun is better than no gun at all for survival, but it isn't as accurate as a rifle and has a much shorter effective range. If there are big game animals in your region, a light and accurate big-game repeating rifle can be a valuable survival weapon. In an area where only small game is available, the most functional caliber would be a .22 long-rifled cartridge.

If only one firearm is to be purchased as a survival weapon, an excellent choice would be the combination gun. This gun has a

.22 long-rifle barrel over either a .410 or 20 gauge shotgun barrel. The .22 over the 20 gauge, the first choice, would be a very practical foraging gun. With high speed .22s and #6 shot for the 20 gauge, a person could comfortably provide meat for a long time in a game-rich wilderness.

If you know the types of game animal in your locality, you can purchase appropriate sporting rifles. In any event, most game (including big game like deer) is actually killed at ranges under 60 yards.

Caring for Firearms

Firearms require a certain amount of care if they are to remain in good working order. Naturally a gun should never be used as a club, hammer, or pry bar. Guns should be kept clean. If possible, cover them when they are not in use. Keep the action, receiver walls, bolt and assembly, and especially the barrel, clean and free from oil, dirt, snow, and mud. If the barrel is obstructed by mud, snow, or any foreign substance, clean it out before shooting. *Never* try to shoot out an obstruction; the barrel will burst.

Don't overoil the gun. Only a few drops on moving parts are needed. In extreme cold, use no oil at all.

A piece of cloth pulled through the barrel on a string is a handy substitute for a ramrod and cleaning patch. If the barrel must have a thorough cleaning and there is no powder solvent, pour boiling water through it from the breech. Mop up the excess water by pulling a cloth on a string through the barrel, and the hot barrel will dry itself.

Weapons sweat when they are brought from extreme cold into a heated room; then when they are taken out again into the cold, the film of condensation freezes. This ice may seriously affect the operation, so leave weapons outdoors or store them in unheated rooms. If your room is not greatly warmer than the outside temperature, you may bring the gun inside, but place it at or near floor level, where the temperature is lowest. When you take a weapon into a heated shelter for cleaning, remove all condensed moisture before cleaning. The metal parts may sweat for an hour.

If a part becomes frozen, do not force it. Warm it slightly, if possible, and move it gradually until it is unfrozen. If it cannot be warmed, try to remove all visible ice or snow and move it gradually until action is restored.

Before loading a gun, always move the action back and forth a few times to ensure that it is free and to check the ammunition.

Hunting and Stalking

- Carry the gun in such a way that if you fall it will not be damaged and you will not be shot.
- Get as close as possible to the game before shooting. Unless it is impossible to secure a clean kill by closer stalking, never attempt to kill by shooting more than 100 yards. Make sure of your first shot: it may be your last at that particular animal, and ammunition should be conserved.
- Don't shoot rapid-fire. One shot does the job if aimed properly.
- Fire from as steady a position as possible. The prone position is best for a steady shot, but sitting or kneeling positions may have to be used. Use a rest such as a log or stone for the barrel whenever possible, but put your hand between the rest and the gun barrel or the gun will shoot wild. Never fire offhand unless you have no time to take another position.
- Aim at a vital spot. The shoulder or chest is probably the best shot for medium and large game. Do not shoot unless a vital spot is open.

Figure 21-1. Vital spots. *U.S. Air Force.*

191

- Do not trust your first shot, even if game appears to have fallen dead. Reload immediately, but keep your eye on the game.
- Hunting with a handgun is difficult at best. It requires careful stalking and a well-aimed shot at a vital spot.
- If necessary, use both hands on the gun to get a steady shot.
- Look for blood if game runs away after the first shot. If you find blood, wait 10 to 30 minutes before following. Wounded game will lie down and stiffen if given time.

Axes and Knives

Your cutting tools are important aids to survival in any environment. For best results, use them and care for them properly.

When you use an axe, don't try to cut through a tree with one blow. Rhythm and aim are more important than force. Too much power behind a swing interferes with your aim. When the axe is swung properly, its weight will provide all the power you need.

Before chopping, clear away all obstructions. A branch, vine, or bush can deflect an axe onto your foot or leg. Remember—an axe can be a wicked weapon.

A broken handle is difficult to remove from the head of the axe. Usually the most convenient method is to burn it out. For a single-bit axe, bury the blade in the ground up to the handle, and burn a fire over it. For a double-bit blade, dig a little trench, lay the middle of the axe over it, cover both bits with earth, and build a fire.

If you have to improvise a new handle, save time and trouble by making a straight handle instead of a curved one like the original. Use a piece of young, straight hardwood without knots. Whittle it roughly into shape and finish it by shaving. Split the end of the handle that fits into the axe head. After it is fitted, pound a thin, dry hardwood wedge into the split. Use the axe awhile, pound the wedge in again, then trim it off flush with the axe.

Your survival kit may include a file or a whetstone. If you don't have a sharpening tool, look for a natural whetstone. You will need it to sharpen your knives and axes. Any sandstone will sharpen tools, but a gray, somewhat clayey sandstone gives better results than a pure quartz. You can recognize quartz instantly by scratching your knife blade with it—quartz is the only common mineral that will bite into steel, cutting a bright groove with every grain. If you don't find sandstone, look for granite or any glittering, crystalline rock except marble. If you use granite, rub two pieces of the stone together until they are smooth before you use one as a grindstone.

Axes can be sharpened best by using both file and whetstone, but a stone alone will keep the axe usable. Use the file every few days, the whetstone after each use. Always push the file away from the blade, wetting the axe with water. Put a finer edge on your axe with the whetstone. Move the stone with a circular motion, from the middle of the blade to the edge

One of the most valuable items in any survival situation is a knife, since it has a great number of uses. Unless the knife is kept sharp, however, it will fall far short of its potential. A knife should be sharpened only with a stone. Repeated use of a file rapidly removes steel from the blade. A circular motion of the stone applied to alternate sides of the blade will put a good cutting edge on the knife.

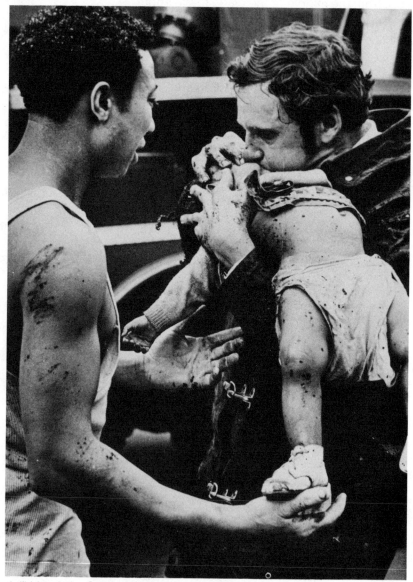

Artificial respiration. *Copyright 1970 by Buffalo Courier-Express. Photo by Ron Moscati.*

22. FIRST AID AND EMERGENCY CARE

Disasters place a special premium on first aid. The general principles that guide all first-aid work still apply, and the same skills are needed, but a major emergency adds new problems and new urgency to the first-aid task. Some of these problems are:

- The number of people requiring first aid treatment may be very large.
- Professional medical care may be unavailable for a long time.
- Normal facilities may be impaired—water supply, heat, light, communications, even shelter.
- Disaster conditions may produce panic, which seriously interferes with emergency care of the injured.

Because a physician or a nurse cannot always be with every disaster victim, your life and the lives of others may depend upon how much you know about first aid and emergency care.

First aid is the emergency or lifesaving care given to a sick or injured person when a medically trained person is not immediately available. It is important that everyone know how to apply lifesaving first-aid measures.

This chapter is designed to be a guide when an emergency arises. For this reason, it contains only essential information about emergencies that you may face and should be able to handle.

You would do well to keep a good first-aid book available at all times as a reference.

Basic Diagnostic Signs

The first aider has indicators available to him in the form of diagnostic signs or symptoms which aid in evaluating a victim's condition. A sign is something the first aider sees, hears, or feels—for example, a pale face, no respiration, cold skin. A symptom is something that the victim tells about himself; that is, he feels nauseous, his back hurts, he has no sensation in the extremities. First aiders learn many signs and symptoms and should learn to combine them into a meaningful diagnosis of the victim's condition. A brief overview of the important diagnostic signs follows.

PULSE

The normal pulse rate for adults is 60 to 80 beats per minute; a normal rate for children is 80 to 100 beats per minute. The pulse is normally taken at the carotid artery on the neck. The pulse can be absent (indicating cardiac arrest), rapid but weak (indicating shock or diabetic coma), or rapid and bounding (indicating fright or hypertension).

RESPIRATION

The normal respiratory rate for adults is about 15 breaths per minute; for children, 20 to 25 breaths per minute; and for infants, 25 to 35 breaths per minute. Respiration may be heard or felt at the nose and mouth, and the chest can be seen rising and falling. Respiration can be absent, gasping, and labored (airway obstruction or heart disease), or accompanied by bright red, frothy blood (lung damage).

TEMPERATURE

Normal body temperature is 98.6°F. In emergency care, temperature is estimated by feel, using the back of the hand on the victim's skin. The skin can be hot and dry (indicating heat stroke or high fever), cool and clammy (indicating shock), or cool and dry (indicating exposure to cold).

SKIN COLOR

Skin color is a useful sign for lightly pigmented people. Skin color can be red (indicating high blood pressure, heart attack, or carbon monoxide poisoning), white (indicating shock or heart attack), or blue (indicating asphyxia or some types of poisoning). For people with dark pigmentation, bluish coloration may be noted around the fingernail beds or inside the lips of the mouth.

PUPILS OF THE EYES

The pupils of the eyes are normally equal in size and constrict (become smaller) when exposed to light. Pupils can be dilated (indicating unconsciousness, fright, or cardiac arrest), constricted (indicating drug use), or unequal (indicating head injury or stroke).

STATE OF CONSCIOUSNESS

The normal person is alert, oriented, and responsive to vocal and physical stimuli. A person's state of consciousness may range from normal to mildly confused, disoriented, or unconscious.

INABILITY TO MOVE ON COMMAND

The normal, conscious person can move his body when requested to do so. A person may not be able to move his legs (indicating injury to the spinal cord below the neck), his arms (indicating injury to the spinal cord in the neck), or one side of his body (indicating stroke or head injury with brain damage).

REACTION TO PHYSICAL STIMULATION

The normal person can feel someone touch his body. A person may have no sensation or a numb feeling in arms and/or legs or certain parts of the body. Damage to the spinal cord may be implicated.

MEDICAL IDENTIFICATION SYMBOLS

People with special medical problems (for example, diabetes, epilepsy, or acute allergic reactions) frequently wear a medical identification symbol on which the nature of the problem is indicated. These are usually worn as a bracelet or necklace but may be carried in card form in a purse or wallet. If the wearer is involved in an accident in which he cannot talk, these symbols can give valuable information about the wearer and the type of care he needs.

Lifesaving Measures

The Basic Procedures

When you approach a victim to administer first aid, follow these steps in the order indicated:
1. Examine promptly and calmly for—
   a. absence of breathing:
      (1) Look for no movement of the chest.
      (2) Feel for no air from the nose or mouth.
      (3) Listen for no air from the nose or mouth.
   b. absence of heartbeat: feel for absence of pulse with the tips of your fingers (not thumb) on the victim's neck at the side of the windpipe (carotid artery).

197

c. presence of bleeding: look for blood flow; spurting blood means bleeding from an artery (not vein or capillary).
2. Apply lifesaving measures instantly:
   a. If there is no sign of breathing, open the airway.
   b. If there is still no sign of breathing, start artificial respiration.
   c. If there is no pulse, or if the pulse is very weak and irregular, start cardiopulmonary resuscitation (if trained).
   d. If there is bleeding, apply direct pressure.
3. Reexamine immediately for—
   a. signs of shock. Early signs are restlessness, thirst, pale skin, rapid heartbeat. The victim may be excited or appear calm and very tired; he may be sweating, even though his skin is cool and clammy.
   b. signs of shock become worse: fast breaths or gasps; staring into space; blotchy or bluish skin, especially around the mouth.
4. Apply shock prevention and control measures. Dress and bandage wounds to prevent infection.

The Important "DO NOTS"

To act incorrectly can be just as serious or fatal as not administering lifesaving first aid at all. Therefore, remember these important "DO NOTS":

- Do not let the victim remain on his back if he is unconscious or has a face or neck wound (He can choke on vomitus, blood, or other fluids).
- Do not pull or tear clothing from the victim.
- Do not touch or try to clean dirty wounds, including burns.
- Do not remove dressings and bandages once they have been placed over a wound.
- Do not loosen a tourniquet once it has been applied.
- Do not move a victim who has a fracture until it has been properly splinted—unless he must be removed from imminent danger.
- Do not give fluids to a victim who is unconscious, nauseated, or vomiting or has an abdominal or neck wound.
- Do not permit the victim's head to be lower than his body when he has a head injury.
- Do not try to push protruding intestines or brain tissue back into a wound.
- Do not put any medication on burns.

198

- Do not attempt first aid measures that are unnecessary or beyond your capabilities.

Artificial Respiration

WHAT TO DO

1. Place on his back the person who has stopped breathing.
2. Open the airway by tilting the head back, placing one hand on the victim's forehead, and pinching the nose; place your other hand under the victim's neck (chin-up position). If a rolled blanket or pillow is readily available, place it under victim's shoulders to help maintain this position.
3. Take a deep breath, make a tight seal around the victim's mouth, and blow air into the victim's mouth until the chest rises. If the chest doesn't rise, suspect a foreign object in the throat. For adults, quickly give four full breaths initially, removing your mouth between breaths to allow air to come out of the victim's mouth.
4. After the initial four breaths, establish a rhythm of 12 to 15 breaths per minute (one breath every 5 seconds). The rhythm is not as important as the volume of air—you must blow until you see the chest rise. If the stomach becomes distended, press it to force air out. The victim will likely belch and may vomit. If the victim vomits, turn his head to one side, remove the vomitus, and continue with resuscitation efforts.
5. For infants, seal your mouth around both the mouth and nose. *Gently* inflate the chest until the chest rises (only small puffs are necessary) at the rate of 20 to 30 breaths per minute (one every 3 seconds); excessive pressure can cause lung damage.

Transporting the Injured

WHAT TO DO

1. Determine carefully the type and seriousness of the injuries and the condition of the injured person.
2. Give complete emergency treatment before moving the injured. Before transporting any sick or injured person,
   a. bleeding should be stopped;
   b. breathing should be established;
   c. fractures should be splinted;
   d. shock should be treated; and
   e. all other lifesaving methods should be completed.

199

3. Be gentle in moving the injured person. Have enough help to assure safe moving.
4. Always carry a stretcher to an injured person, not the person to the stretcher.
5. Stretchers should be used for the more seriously injured persons and for transporting the injured over a long distance.
6. Be sure the person will not slip or fall from the stretcher while being carried. Belts or strong cloth bindings such as sheets may be used to secure the person to a stretcher.
7. Always use a two-man carry in preference to a one-man carry.
8. The various hand carries should not be used unless the person needs only slight support for short distances, or in emergencies, when delay will endanger life (e.g., fire or explosion).

WHAT NOT TO DO

Do not be in a hurry to move an injured person.

Emergency Treatments

The following is an alphabetical listing of various medical emergencies, together with suggestions for *what to do* and *what not to do*. In most instances, the procedures suggested are for initial treatment only—steps to consider when it is impossible to get the victim immediate professional care.

Abscess/Boil

WHAT TO DO

1. Leave it alone if it is closed; wait for it to open by itself.
2. Cover it with a sterile or clean dressing if it is draining.
3. Apply hot packs if possible.
4. Give aspirin for pain.
5. When possible, keep clothing away from the area to prevent spreading infection.

WHAT NOT TO DO

1. Do not squeeze a pimple, boil, or carbuncle.
2. Do not prick it with a pin or needle.
3. Do not lance it or open it.

Appendicitis

WHAT TO DO

1. Check for these signs and symptoms:

a. Pain in lower right or upper part of abdomen.

b. Possible nausea or vomiting.

c. Fever (seldom present at first).

2. An ice bag over appendix area may relieve discomfort.

3. Get the victim to a medical-treatment facility immediately.

WHAT NOT TO DO

1. Do not give food or water.

2. Do not give a laxative.

3. Do not heat the abdomen.

Asthma Attack

WHAT TO DO

1. Place the victim in a comfortable sitting position.

2. Reassure the victim.

3. Determine if he has his own medication.

4. Administer the medication only after checking with victim as to exact dosage and proper administration.

Bites

Mammal

WHAT TO DO

1. Wash the wound thoroughly with soap and water.

2. Catch the animal and confine it for 14 days (if practical) for observation in case of rabies.

Bee, Wasp, Hornet

WHAT TO DO

1. Remove the stinger (bees only).

2. Apply ice or cold cloths to the sting.

3. For victims who are allergic to certain insects, use a constricting band to keep poison from spreading. Use epinephrine quickly, if available.

4. Apply calamine lotion to soothe the pain.

Scorpion

WHAT TO DO

1. Apply a constricting band above the sting on the side toward the heart. Remove it after it has been in place about 5 minutes.

2. Apply an ice pack, if available; otherwise, apply cold, wet cloths to the sting.

3. Keep the person warm and quiet.
4. Keep the affected arm or leg lower than the rest of the body for about 2 hours.

Snake

WHAT TO DO

1. Immobilize the victim immediately, keeping the injured part lower than the rest of the body. Any activity will stimulate the spread of poison.
2. Remove rings, watches, and bracelets.
3. Apply a constricting band above the swelling caused by the bite. It should be tight, but not tight enough to stop circulation altogether.
4. Make an incision, no more than ⅛ inch deep or more than ½ inch long, lengthwise through the fang marks. Press around the cut to make it bleed.
5. Apply suction to the wound with the device found in a snake-bite kit. If no kit is available, use your mouth and spit out the blood. Rinse your mouth out between sections. Cutting and suction is of no value, however, unless it is done within 30 minutes of the bite.
6. If swelling continues past the constricting band, put another one on past the swelling and loosen the first band.
7. Treat the victim for shock.

WHAT NOT TO DO

1. Do not cut if the bite is near a major blood vessel.
2. Do not give the victim any stimulants or alcohol.
3. Do not cut and suck if the victim can receive medical care within 1 or 2 hours.

Spider (Black Widow)

WHAT TO DO

1. Keep the victim quiet.
2. Elevate his hips and legs as if you were treating him for shock.
3. Keep the affected part down, below the level of the victim's heart.
4. Apply a cold pack to the bite.

Bleeding

WHAT TO DO

1. Apply a dressing or pad directly over the wound.

2. Apply direct, even pressure—use your bare hand if necessary when bleeding is serious and a dressing is not immediately available.
3. Leave the dressing in place.
4. Continue pressure by applying a bandage.
5. Secure the bandage in place—check to be sure it is not so tight that it cuts off circulation.
6. If the bleeding is from a limb, elevate the limb above heart level—except where there is a possible broken bone.
7. Treat the victim for shock.
8. If blood soaks through the dressing, do not remove it; simply apply more dressings.
9. If you are unsuccessful in stopping the bleeding, apply pressure to either the brachial or femoral artery.

WHAT NOT TO DO

Do not use a tourniquet unless it is impossible to stop excessive life-threatening bleeding by any other method.

Blisters

WHAT TO DO

1. Wash the blister area clean.
2. Sterilize a needle.
3. Open the blister from its edge with the needle.
4. Gently squeeze out the fluid and cover the blister with a dressing.
5. Keep it clean.

WHAT NOT TO DO

If there is no pain, do not open blisters. *Never* break blisters that form over serious burns.

Burns

WHAT TO DO

1. Treat the victim for shock.
2. Relieve pain as best you can. Apply cold water to minor burns.
3. Prevent infection: cover the burned area with a dry sterile dressing or clean cloth.
4. Encourage the victim to take liquids to replace fluid lost from his body. Give him a water, salt, and baking soda solution: 1 teaspoonful salt and ½ teaspoonful baking soda to 1 quart water.

1. Do not pull clothes over the burned area.
2. Do not remove pieces of cloth that stick to a burn.
3. Do not try to clean the burn.
4. Do not break blisters.
5. Do not use grease, ointment, petroleum jelly, or any type of medication on second- or third-degree burns.
6. Do not use iodine or antiseptics on burns.
7. Do not touch a burn with anything except a sterile or clean dressing.
8. Until it is absolutely necessary to do so, do not change the dressings initially applied. (They may be left in place five to seven days.)

Chills

WHAT TO DO

1. Put the person to bed.
2. Keep the person warm.

Choking

WHAT TO DO

1. Give four quick blows to the victim's back while holding his head down.
2. If back blows fail to dislodge an obstructing object, place yourself behind a sitting or standing victim and wrap your arms around his waist. Make a fist and place it thumb-side in just above the navel and below the rib cage. Clasp the fist with your other hand and press it into the upper section of the abdomen, thrusting upward quickly—four times. Then, check the victim's mouth for foreign objects.
3. If the victim is lying down, roll him on his side so that he faces you with his chest against your knees. Deliver four sharp blows to the back. If this is unsuccessful, place the victim face up. Kneel beside his hips, and with one of your hands on top of the other, place the heel of the bottom hand on the victim's abdomen just above the navel and below the rib cage. Press the diaphragm four times with quick upward thrusts. Finally, try to remove the obstructing object with your finger. Repeat these steps until the object is expelled.

Common Cold

WHAT TO DO

1. For adults, give two aspirin every four hours; for children, one aspirin every four hours.
2. Give ample amounts of fluids to drink—preferably fruit juices, if available.
3. Make sure the patient gets as much rest as possible.
4. Administer a nasal spray (Neosynephrine) to decongest eustachian tube.

Convulsion / Epilepsy

WHAT TO DO

Keep the person from hurting himself.

WHAT NOT TO DO

Do not attempt to restrain the person having the attack, except to prevent him from injuring himself.

Croup

WHAT TO DO

Inhale steam from boiling water provides the best means of relief.

Diabetic Emergency

WHAT TO DO

1. Put the victim to bed.
2. Prop him in a partial sitting-up position.
3. Keep him warm.
4. Give a sugar cube or other sugar source to insulin shock victim.
5. If you are unable to distinguish between a diabetic coma and insulin shock and sugar is available, have the victim take the sugar. It cannot appreciably hurt a victim in diabetic coma and may save the life of a victim in insulin shock.

Diarrhea

WHAT TO DO

1. Withhold any food for 24 hours.
2. Give water if the person does not also have nausea and vomiting.

3. If diarrhea persists for 2 to 3 days, give the person a sugar-salt solution: dissolve 1 level teaspoonful of salt and 1½ table-spoonfuls of sugar in a quart of water. Ginger ale or Seven-up may also be used.
4. Watch for dehydration.
5. When diarrhea stops, give warm liquid or soft diet. Progress diet slowly, starting with such foods as bananas, rice, and applesauce.
6. To prevent infecting yourself and others, be extremely careful in handling the stools of a person who has diarrhea.

Earache

WHAT TO DO

1. Apply a hot-water bottle to the affected ear.
2. Give aspirin for pain.
3. Give a decongestant (Neosynephrine nose spray) to decongest eustachian tube.

WHAT NOT TO DO

Do not use any kind of ear drop in an ear that is discharging fluid.

Emotional Problem

(See "Psychological First Aid," p. 221.)

Eye Injury

WHAT TO DO

1. Use the corner of a clean handkerchief to remove foreign objects from the lower lid.
2. If a foreign object under the upper lid cannot readily be seen, grasp the upper lid and lashes, pull them down, place a match over the lid, and pull the lid up and back over the match while the victim looks down. Look for foreign objects on the upper lid. Gently remove them with a corner of a clean handkerchief.
3. If it is necessary to bandage one eye, cover both to minimize eye movement.

WHAT NOT TO DO

1. Never rub an eye that has a foreign body in it.
2. If an object has penetrated the eyeball, do not remove it; fluid may be lost, resulting in permanent blindness.

3. Do not exert pressure directly on a lacerated eyeball.
4. Do not replace an extruded eyeball.

Fever

1. Determine how high the temperature is.
2. Put the person to bed in a cool environment, and encourage him to drink fluids.
3. Give two aspirin every four hours.
4. When the fever is severe (more than 102°F in adults, more than 103°F in children), give a sponge bath or apply cool compresses.
5. When fever and chills occur alternately, refer to section on chills.

Fracture

1. Look for bleeding and control it.
2. When in doubt, treat a suspicious injury as a fracture.
3. Apply a splint at the site of the accident. Never move the person before splinting, unless delay would further endanger his life.
4. Splint securely enough to prevent any voluntary or involuntary movement at the point of fracture.
5. Prevent shock, further injury, and infection.
6. Check splint ties frequently to be sure the splint does not interfere with the circulation of blood.

Figure 22-1. A toe is a good splint for another toe—or a leg for a leg, or a finger for a finger.

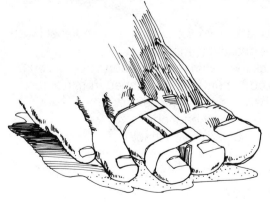

Frostbite

WHAT TO DO

1. Rapidly thaw frostbitten parts of the victim's body by—
   a. placing the affected part next to a warm part of your body;
   b. placing the frostbitten part of the body in lukewarm water (about 103°–107°F).
2. Handle the affected parts with great care and gentleness.

WHAT NOT TO DO

1. Do not rub the affected part.
2. Do not use hot water.
3. Do not use a hot water bottle or heat lamps.
4. Do not disturb blisters if they develop.
5. Do not rub frostbitten parts with ice or snow.
6. Do not attempt to thaw deep frostbite. There is less damage walking on feet when they are frozen than after they are thawed.
7. Do not thaw if the victim has to go back out into the cold, which may refreeze the affected areas.

Headache

WHAT TO DO

1. Give 2 aspirins every four hours for adults; one aspirin every four hours for children.
2. Have the victim rest for a few hours.
3. If the headache persists, put the person to bed.
4. Apply cold compresses to the forehead and back of the neck.

Head Injury

WHAT TO DO

1. Inspect for scalp wounds. If there are no scalp wounds, check for other signs and symptoms:
   a. Is or has the victim recently been unconscious?
   b. Has blood or other fluid escaped from his nose or ears?
   c. Does he have a slow pulse?
   d. Does he have a headache?
   e. Is he nauseated or vomiting?
   f. Has he had convulsions?
   g. Is he breathing very slowly?
2. Give first aid.

3. Leave any protruding brain tissue as it is, and place a moist sterile dressing over this tissue.
4. Position the victim so that his head is higher than his body.

Do not remove or disturb any foreign matter in the wound.

Heart Emergency

1. Administer medication (nitroglycerine) if the victim has any.
2. Place the victim in a comfortable position, usually partially sitting up, particularly if shortness of breath accompanies the heart attack. Loosen tight clothing.
3. Reassure the victim, and stay with him.
4. When he is able to eat, allow him a soft diet (preferably salt-free) and about one quart of fluids per day.
5. If the heart has stopped, administer cardiopulmonary resuscitation if you are trained to do so.
6. Keep onlookers away.

1. Do not allow the victim to assist in moving himself; he needs complete rest.
2. Give no stimulants.

Heat Exhaustion

1. Lay the victim down in a cool place; cover him if he gets too cold.
2. Give him cool, salted water to sip: 1 teaspoonful of salt to a glass of water, every 15 minutes, over a period of about 1 hour.
3. Care for the victim as if he were in shock.

Heat Stroke

1. Undress the person, and put him in the coolest available area.
2. Sponge his body freely with water or alcohol to reduce his temperature to 102°F or less.

3. To hold his temperature at 102°F or less, you may place damp sheets or blankets over the victim. Fanning the body may be useful.

WHAT NOT TO DO

Do not give stimulants such as coffee or tea.

Hernia

WHAT TO DO

1. Have the victim lie flat on his back with his knees drawn up. In this position, the loops of a bowel and other abdominal contents are more likely to return to the abdomen, causing the swelling to disappear.
2. If number 1 fails, have the person again lie on his back and apply cold compresses to the site of the hernia.
3. If numbers 1 and 2 both fail to reduce the hernia, have the person turn over on his stomach and bring the knees under his chest so that the buttocks are raised. Have him remain in this position for a few minutes to see if the hernia will be reduced.

WHAT NOT TO DO

1. Do not attempt to push the hernia back into place with the fingers. This may cause serious damage.
2. Do not give any laxative or cathartic unless approved by a physician when communication is possible.

Hypothermia (Exposure)

The inner core of the body is chilled so that the body cannot generate heat to stay warm.

WHAT TO DO

1. Bring the victim into a warm room as quickly as possible.
2. Remove wet clothing.
3. Wrap the victim in prewarmed blankets, put him in a warm tub of water, or have him lie next to one or between two people for body warmth.
4. Give artificial respiration if necessary.
5. If the victim is conscious, give him a warm drink.

WHAT NOT TO DO

Do not give alcohol

Nausea and Vomiting

WHAT TO DO

1. Determine the cause if possible.
2. Put the person to bed.
3. If the cause can be determined, refer to the appropriate section for further instructions.
4. Give warm liquid only when it can be tolerated.
5. If vomiting persists, encourage the person to take as much fluid as possible to prevent dehydration.
6. Start soft foods after liquids have been retained for 24 hours.

Nosebleed

WHAT TO DO

1. Place the person in a sitting position and have him breathe through his mouth.
2. Most nosebleeds will stop spontaneously. But if bleeding continues, try the following measures:
   a. Gently grasp the lower end of the nose between the thumb and index finger, firmly press the sides of the nose against the center for 5 minutes.
   b. Release pressure gradually.
   c. Apply cold cloths to the back of the neck or over the nose.
3. If bleeding persists, plug the bleeding nostrils with a small strip of gauze rolled up loosely. (Leave part of roll sticking out of the nose so that it can be easily removed later.)

Pain

WHAT TO DO

1. Locate the pain area.
2. Determine the severity of the pain.
3. Determine, if possible, the cause.
4. If the cause can be determined, refer to the appropriate section for further instructions.
5. When the cause cannot be determined, apply cold compresses to area of pain.
6. Give aspirin as directed on the bottle.

Poisoning

WHAT TO DO

1. Dilute the poison with water or milk.

2. Induce vomiting (by administering syrup of ipecac, or by tick-ling the back of the throat to aid in removing poisons from the stomach. *But,* vomiting should not be induced when—
   a. strong acids or alkalis are swallowed (these will reinjure the esophagus if regurgitated);
   b. petroleum products are swallowed (a serious pneumonia could result if these substances are aspirated into the lungs);
   c. the victim is not fully conscious (he might aspirate vomitus into the lungs);
   d. the victim has convulsed (vomitus might bring on more convulsions); or
   e. the victim is pregnant (during the late months labor may be precipitated).

Radiation Sickness

WHAT TO DO

1. Look for early signs and symptoms: lack of appetite, nausea and vomiting, fatigue and weakness, headache. Later symp-toms may be: sore mouth, loss of hair, bleeding gums, bleed-ing under the skin, diarrhea. These same symptoms may be caused by other diseases, however; and not everyone who has radiation sickness shows all these symptoms, or shows them all at once.
2. If the victim has a headache or general discomfort, give him 1 or 2 aspirin every 3 to 4 hours (half a tablet for a child under 12).
3. If the victim is nauseous, give him "motion sickness" tablets, if they are available.
4. If there is vomiting or diarrhea, the victim should drink slowly several glasses of a salt-soda solution each day (1 teaspoonful of salt and ½ teaspoonful of baking soda to a quart of cool wa-ter), plus bouillon or fruit juices. If available, a mixture of kaolin and pectin should be given for diarrhea.
5. If the victim's mouth is sore or his gums are bleeding, prepare a mouthwash for him: ½ teaspoonful of salt to a quart of water.
6. Whatever his symptoms, the patient should be kept lying down, comfortably warm, and resting.
7. Remember that radiation sickness is not contagious; one per-son cannot "catch it" from another.

Shock

1. Keep the person lying down.
2. Keep his head lower than his legs and hips if there is no chest or head injury.
3. Have the head and shoulders slightly raised when the victim has a chest or head injury or has difficulty in breathing.
4. Keep the victim from chilling.
5. Encourage fluids by mouth if the victim is conscious. Use a solution of 1 teaspoonful of salt and ½ teaspoonful of baking soda to a quart of water. Give ½ glassful every 15 minutes.

WHAT NOT TO DO

1. Never attempt to give fluids to an unconscious person.
2. Alcohol should not be used as a stimulant.

Skin Rash

WHAT TO DO

1. To relieve itching, apply a compress soaked in cool soda solution: 3 teaspoons of baking soda to a glass of cool water.
2. For rashes with small pimples or eruptions, cover generously with a paste of bicarbonate of soda.
3. Caution the person not to scratch or rub the inflamed area.
4. Calamine lotion applied may soothe.

Stroke (Apoplexy)

WHAT TO DO

1. Put the victim to bed, propped up on pillows if that will make him more comfortable.
2. When breathing is difficult, turn the victim's face to one side so that fluid may drain from his mouth.
3. Remove any loose dental bridges or false teeth.
4. Be careful what you say in front of the victim, even if he appears unconscious; he may be able to hear what is being said. Reassure the victim; don't frighten him.
5. Keep the victim quiet and warm.

WHAT NOT TO DO

Do not allow the victim's tongue to block his air passage.

Toothache

1. If oil of cloves or toothache drops are available, apply some to a small piece of cotton and gently pack it into the tooth cavity. Repeat two or three times daily.
2. Ice packs or hot packs may provide relief. Apply packs to the cheek next to the aching tooth.
3. Aspirin may be used to relieve the pain. (Do not suck it.)

Unconsciousness

WHAT TO DO

1. When the victim is flushed (red faced) with a strong, slow pulse:
   a. Lay him down with his head slightly raised above the level of the rest of his body.
   b. Apply a cold, wet cloth to his head.
   c. If breathing stops, start artificial respiration.
2. When victim is pale, cold and clammy to touch, with a weak pulse:
   a. Lay him down with his head slightly lower than the rest of his body.
   b. Keep him warm.
   c. If breathing stops, start artificial respiration.
3. When the victim has a bluish face, weak pulse, and irregular breathing:
   a. Lay him down.
   b. Keep him warm.
   c. Start artificial respiration immediately if breathing stops.

WHAT NOT TO DO

1. Do not give stimulants.
2. Do not give food or drink.
3. Do not move the victim (except to remove him from imminent danger).

Vomiting

WHAT TO DO

1. No fluids or solids for 2–4 hours.
2. Give ginger ale or Seven-Up in small quantities.
3. Watch for dehydration.

4. Start progressing diet 24 hours after last vomiting. Start with bananas, rice, and applesauce.

Wounds

Abdominal Wound

The victim has a deep puncture wound or is eviscerated.

WHAT TO DO

1. Leave protruding organs as they are and place a sterile dressing over them. Keep the dressing moist.
2. Secure dressings in place with bandages, but do not apply them tightly.
3. Leave the victim on his back with his head turned to one side. Because he will probably vomit, watch him closely to prevent choking.

WHAT NOT TO DO:

Do not allow the victim to take anything by mouth.

Chest Wound (Sucking)

Air is being sucked into the chest cavity, collapsing the lung on the injured side.

WHAT TO DO

1. If possible, have the victim breathe out and hold his breath while you seal the wound.
2. Seal the wound airtight with a plastic wrapper.
3. Place a dressing and a bandage over the plastic wrapper.
4. If the victim wants to lie down, encourage him to lie on his injured side. He may find sitting more comfortable; if so, allow him to do so.

Face/Neck Wound

Bleeding is usually profuse and hard to control because of many blood vessels in area.

WHAT TO DO

1. Stop bleeding that is causing obstruction of the upper airway.
2. Clear the airway with your fingers, removing blood, mucus, any pieces of broken teeth or bone, bits of flesh, and dentures.
3. Either have the victim sit leaning forward with head down to permit drainage from his mouth, or place him on his abdomen

with head turned to the side to permit drainage from his mouth.

Suturing an Open Wound

If the wound is gaping, it will have to be brought together. This is done most easily with a butterfly bandage. However, for deep cuts in fingers and other places subject to much movement, a stitch may be better.

You can buy sterile suture packages that have cutting needles with nylon thread attached. Size 3-0 needles can be used everywhere except on the face, where a size 5-0 is recommended. The 5-0 is finer and has less tendency to leave a scar.

The wound is first washed with soap and water, dried, then sutured. (The needle is held with a small hemostat, a miniature, self-locking, needle-nose clamp.) This is done without Novocain, because nerves are often cut along with other tissue, and the pain of the sewing needle is not as bad as one might think.

The suture is taken through the skin, never deeper into the underlying fat or muscle. By not going any deeper, no vital structure will ever be encountered. The only possible source of difficulty might be in hitting a blood vessel. If this happens, simply pull the suture clear through and out of the skin and take it in another spot a little above or below the one that caused the trouble. The bleeding will stop when pressure is applied for a minute or so. Never suture close to an eyelid; the healing may pull the skin into a distorted position and cause later difficulties.

Once the stitch is taken, tie the suture and cut it with a scalpel blade. The ends are left a quarter of an inch long to facilitate removal in 7 days. The hemostat can substitute as a pair of tweezers to remove the severed stitch.

Medicines and First-Aid Supplies

During many disasters and other emergencies, various medicines and first-aid supplies are sorely needed. The lists that follow detail nearly a hundred items that you should consider keeping on hand in preparation for medical crises.

Medicines

If a chronic illness (e.g., diabetes and hypertension) requires daily medication, a supply should be kept at home in case a disaster occurs, cutting off sources of supply. Consult with your physician

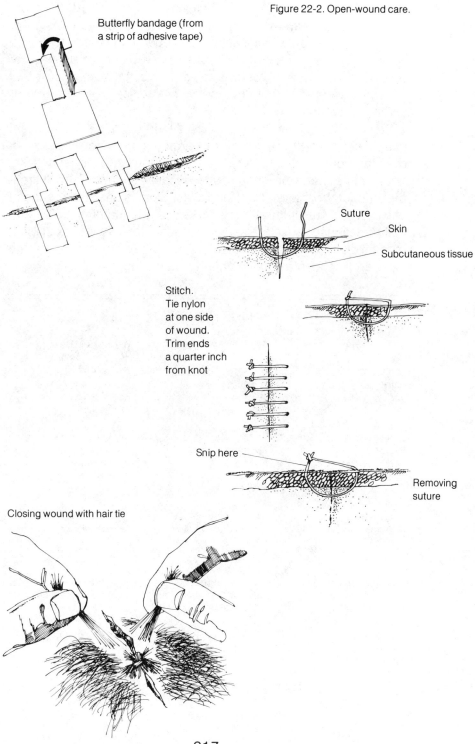

Figure 22-2. Open-wound care.

Butterfly bandage (from a strip of adhesive tape)

Suture

Skin

Subcutaneous tissue

Stitch.
Tie nylon
at one side
of wound.
Trim ends
a quarter inch
from knot

Snip here

Removing
suture

Closing wound with hair tie

217

for details on the quantity and shelf life of any medicines needed. If your physician knows the purpose of the drugs you desire for storage in the event of a disaster, he probably will agree to let you have them. He is responsible for the use of any drug he prescribes. If he disapproves of a drug suggested below, or if that drug has been discontinued, follow his advice. He knows your particular needs.

Be very careful with medications. All drugs, taken in sufficient quantities, have the potential for harmful side effects. Misuse of over-the-counter drugs can also have serious consequences. Do not assume that a product is safe because it does not require a prescription from a doctor. Keep all medicines out of the reach of children. Be sure that all containers are adequately labeled and that directions for use are kept with each. Notice the date of expiration for each medicine. If the date has passed or if the medicine looks spoiled, destroy it and obtain a new supply.

TABLE 22-1. SUGGESTED MEDICINES FOR STORAGE

Name of Drug	Adult Dosage	Reason for Use
Achromycin caps	250 mg 4 times daily	Bacterial infections
Ampicillin	250 mg 4 times daily	Bacterial infections
Aspirin	1–2 tablets as needed	Pain, headache
Benadryl	1 capsule every 4 hours	Allergies
Block-Out or Pre-Sun, Paba-film, Pabanol	As directed	Sunscreen agents
Betadine solution	As directed	Antiseptic
Butyn or Pontocaine	As directed	Eye anesthetic
Caladryl lotion	As directed	Itching skin
Cepacol gargle or saltwater	As directed	Sore throat
Compazine	1 tablet every 4 hours	Nausea or vomiting
Cortisone (prednisone)	1 tablet every 4 hours 4 times daily, then taper to 1 tablet every 12 hours for 2 days	Bursitis, allergic reactions
Darvon compound	1 capsule every 4 hours	Pain, headache
Di-Gel liquid	2 tsp every 2 hours	Gas, acid indigestion
Debrox drops	5 drops daily	Ear wax
Fleet enema	As directed	Severe constipation
Gantrisin	4 times daily	Urinary tract infection
Lomotil	2 tablets 3 times daily	Diarrhea
Maalox or Gelusil, Mylanta, Riopan	As directed	Upset stomach
Metamucil	As directed	Bulk laxative for constipation

Name of Drug	Adult Dosage	Reason for Use
Milk of magnesia	As directed	Saline laxative for constipation
Neosporin ointment	2 to 4 times daily	Skin infections
Neosynephrine nasal spray (0.25% for children, 0.5% for adults)	3 times daily	Nasal congestion, sinusitis
Oil of cloves	Few drops as needed	Toothache
Parapectolin	1 or 2 tbsp 4 times daily	Long-acting antihistamine for allergic reactions, stings, and other allergy problems
Robitussin-DM	As directed	Cough control
Seconal	1 at bedtime	Insomnia
Spectrocin or Bacitracin, Cortisporin	Apply 3 to 4 times daily	eye infection
Sudafed tablets	As directed	Decongestant for colds and allergies
Sulfasuxidine	2 or 3 tablets every 4 hours	Dysentery
Syrup of ipecac	½ oz and repeat once if needed; use with water	To induce vomiting in case of ingested poison
Tinactine or Selsun, Desenex	As directed	Antifungal
Triaminic syrup	As directed	Colds, allergies
Tylenol	1 or 2 tablets as needed	Pain, headache
Vaseline Intensive Care Lotion	As needed	Skin dryness
Zinc oxide	As needed	Chapped lips

First-Aid Supplies

TABLE 22-2. SUGGESTED FIRST-AID KIT CONTENTS

First-Aid Item	Use
Activated charcoal	To bind and/or absorb poison
Adhesive bandages (Band-Aids)—different sizes; plastic-coated to avoid sticking	Open wounds
Adhesive tape—1- and 2-inch rolls—1 roll of each size	To hold dressings and bandage in place
Alcohol (70%)—1 pint bottle	For poison ivy; to sterilize; to cool body (except infants)
Alcohol wipes—towelettes—12	To clean hands
Aspirin—5 gr.—1 bottle	Depress pain
Baking soda—small container	In case of delayed medical attention for third-degree burns and/or shock
Bandage—3 × 1-inch rollers	Finger bandages
Bandage—3 × 2-inch rollers	To hold dressings in place
Bulb aspirator	Suck blood and other secretions from back of throat
Calamine lotion—bottle, 4 to 6 ounces	Poison ivy, poison sumac, poison oak, and soothe minor bites and stings
Constriction band made of rubber tubing	Bites and stings
Cotton applicators—1 package	To make swabs
Cotton (sterile) half-ounce package	Swabs
Dimes and nickels	For pay-telephone calls
Elastic wraps (Ace bandages) 2- and 3-inch width, 1 can	To hold dressings
Emergency telephone numbers: doctor, fire and police departments, hospital, poison control center	To reach those who can assist
Epsom salts	For a laxative in case of poisoning
First-aid manual	As a guide on what and what not to do
Flashlight and extra batteries	To examine throat; for vision in darkness
Hot-water bottle	Relief of pain
Ice bag (plastic)	To reduce swelling; for burns; for relief of pain; the bag itself without ice can cover third-degree burns or sucking check wounds
Kerlix gauze rolls—2	To cover wounds
Kwik Kold, 5'' × 10''—2	For instant cold pack
Matches	To sterilize needles, scissors, dressings
Measuring cup and spoons	For measuring
Medicine dropper	To rinse eyes
Needles	To remove splinters
Oil of cloves	To place on cotton for toothache
Paper and pencil	To record information and send messages

First-Aid Item	Use
Paper drinking cups	To give drinks; to cover eye injuries
Penlight	For contraction of eyes; to examine nose and throat
Safety pins—12, various sizes	To tie bandages
Salt (table)—dilute with water before administering	For delayed treatment of shock and burns; for treatment for heat cramps
Scissors—1 pair	Cutting
Sharp knife or razor blade	Cutting
Snakebite kit	Treatment of snakebite
Soap (mild)	Cleaning wounds
Splints—2 or 3, different lengths	Splinting broken arms and legs
Sterile dressings (gauze)—in paper packages, sizes 2 × 2, 4 × 4, 6 × 6 inches	To cover wounds
Sterile eye pads—3 or 4	To cover injured eyes
Sterile gauze (also called rolled gauze)—rolls in widths up to 3 inches, 1 each	To cover wounds
Sterile soap—liquid, 4 to 6 ounces	Cleaning
Sugar cubes—small container	Insulin shock
Syrup of ipecac—6 ounces	To induce vomiting in poison cases
Tackle box	To store and transport supplies listed
Thermometer—1 oral, 1 rectal	To determine body temperature
Tongue blades	To splint broken fingers
Towel	Drying
Triangular bandages—at least 4, with material for making more	Bandages, tourniquet, sling
Tweezers—1 pair	To remove small splinters
Wire ladder splints—1	For splinting fractures

Not Recommended

See Consumers Union, *The Medicine Show*, New York: Pantheon Books, 1974:
Mercurochrome, Merthiolate, iodine
Ammonia—aromatic spirit, inhalant ampules
Boric acid
Over-the-counter burn ointments

Alton L. Thygerson, Study Guide for First-Aid Practices, *Englewood Cliffs, New Jersey: Prentice-Hall, Inc., 1978.*

Psychological First Aid

Many of the disasters discussed in this book are notorious for taking heavy tolls in death and physical injury. However, another kind of injury frequently occurs during disasters: psychological injury, a form of damage to human beings that requires its own kind of first aid.

Psychological first aid really means nothing more than helping people with emotional injuries, whether those injuries result from

221

physical injury or from excessive or unbearable strain on the victim's emotions.

Psychological first aid often goes hand in hand with physical first aid, because a physical injury and the circumstances surrounding it may actually cause an additional emotional injury. On the other hand, psychological injury may occur even when there is no real danger of physical injury. Emotional injuries are not as apparent as physical injuries, but both can be severe, and both need treatment. Unfortunately, the chances of psychological overreaction are somewhat higher just at those times when trained medical personnel are not around to provide reassurance.

In the aftermath of a disaster, you may be working alongside someone who cannot handle the impact of a catastrophe upon his emotions. If he is suffering from pain, shock, and fear of serious injury or even death, he will not likely respond well to joking, indifference, or fearful-tearful attention. Although emotional reactions are temporary, lasting only for minutes, hours, or at the most a few days, they are seriously disabling, often contagious, and may result in danger not only to the emotionally upset person but to others as well. For these reasons, it is very important for you to know that first aid can be applied to injuries of the mind as well as to those of the body, and that you can understand the basic principles of this psychological first aid.

Typical Reactions to Disasters

With few exceptions, all people feel fear in the face of a disaster. In such a situation you should not be surprised if you feel shaky, perspire profusely, and become a little nauseated and confused. These reactions are normal and are no cause for concern. Most people are able to "collect" themselves within a short time. After a while, if you get busy, your heart will stop pounding, your breath will come back, and you will feel less tense.

Some reactions, however, can be easily recognized as abnormal. The following are the most usual types:

- Physical Reactions. Sometimes bodily reactions such as rapid breathing, fast pulse, and shakiness go far beyond mere "butterflies." When these physical symptoms become severe, they may result in violent nausea and vomiting and a kind of psychological paralysis that inhibits the effective performance of the victim's normal duties.

222

- Depressed Reactions. Most people are dazed, shocked, or numb after a disaster; but this condition promptly clears up. Sometimes, however, a person will not be able "to shake it off." He acts as if he were alone in the world. When he moves, if he does, his movements are slow and aimless. He will hardly respond to anyone or anything and will show no emotion at all—only a vacant stare. A person like this is completely helpless and unaware of his surroundings.
- Overactive Reactions. In disaster situations you can expect "running about" and confusion. Some people, however, seem to run about excessively, creating additional confusion and doing things that are of no value or even harmful. They talk a lot, make silly jokes, or may be demanding, critical, and overly confident. You can see them jump from job to job, brush aside any directions, and make a spectacle of themselves.
- Panic Reactions. Perhaps you can easily understand how overwhelming fear can cause some people to act in abnormal ways. You can remember how you have felt or how others have acted when severely frightened. Some people seem to lose all control and do things in a blind, unreasonable way. They may run aimlessly with complete disregard for their safety, may weep so severely that they become exhausted and unable to care for themselves even when their lives depend upon it, or may recklessly go about doing things that make no sense.

You do not need much training to recognize severe abnormal reactions. Some victims, however, will have reactions that are less severe and more difficult to detect. To determine whether or not a person needs help, find out if he is doing something that makes sense and if he is able to perform his duties and take care of himself. Furthermore, you should stop from time to time and carefully assess your own emotional condition. You may need to either slow down or get yourself going.

First-Aid Measures

Table 22-3 lists the typical kinds of disaster reactions and summarizes the most important dos and don'ts of administering psychological first aid. For the most part, these psychological first-aid measures are simple and easy to understand. However, improvisation is in order, just as it is in splinting a fracture. Whether or not you use good judgment depends largely upon your ability to ob-

223

TABLE 22-3. PSYCHOLOGICAL FIRST AID FOR DISASTER REACTIONS

Reactions	Symptoms	Do	Don't

Normal	Trembling
	Muscular tension
	Perspiration
	Nausea
	Mild diarrhea
	Urinary frequency
	Pounding heart
	Rapid breathing
	Anxiety
		Give reassurance
		Provide group
		  identification
		Motivate
		Talk with him
		Observe to see
		  that individual
		  is gaining
		  composure not
		  losing it
			Don't show
			  resentment
			Don't overdo
			  sympathy

Individual Panic
(flight reaction)
	Unreasoning
	  attempt to flee
	Loss of judgment
	Uncontrolled
	  weeping
	Wild running
	  about
		Try kindly
		  firmness at first
		Give something
		  warm to eat or
		  drink
		Get help to
		  isolate, if
		  necessary
		Be empathetic
		Encourage him to
		  talk
		Be aware of your
		  own limitations
			Don't use brutal
			  restraint
			Don't strike
			Don't douse with
			  water
			Don't give
			  sedatives

Depression
(underactive
reactions)
	Stand or sit
	  without moving
	  or talking
	Vacant
	  expression
	Lack of emotional
	  display
		Get contact
		  gently
		Secure rapport
		Get them to tell
		  you what
		  happened
		Be empathetic
		Recognize feelings
		  of resentment
		  in patient and
		  yourself
		Find simple,
		  routine job
		Give warm food,
		  drink
			Don't tell them to
			  "snap out of it"
			Don't overdo pity
			Don't give
			  sedatives
			Don't act
			  resentful

Overactive	Argumentative
	Talk rapidly
	Joke
	  inappropriately
	Make endless
	  suggestions
	Jump from one
	  activity to
	  another
		Let them talk
		  about it
		Find them jobs
		  which require
		  physical effort
		Give warm food,
		  drink
		Supervision
		  necessary
		Be aware of own
		  feelings
			Don't suggest
			  that they are
			  acting
			  abnormally
			Don't give
			  sedatives
			Don't argue
			  with them

Reactions	Symptoms	Do	Don't
Physical (conversion reaction)	Severe nausea and vomiting Can't use some part of the body	Show interest in them Find small job for them to make them forget Make comfortable Get medical help if possible Be aware of own feelings	Don't tell them that there's nothing wrong with them Don't blame Don't ridicule Ignore disability openly

Modified from M 51-400-603-1, Dept. of Non-resident Instruction, Medical Field Service School, Brooke Army Medical Center, Fort Sam Houston, Texas.

serve the casualty and truly understand the needs that have to be met.

Whatever the situation, you will have your own emotional reactions (consciously or unconsciously) toward the victim. These reactions are very important—they can either help or hinder your ability to help him. Especially when you are tired or worried, you may very easily become impatient with the person who seems to be "dragging his heels" or "making mountains out of molehills." You may even feel resentful toward him for being such a nuisance. At times when many injured lie about you, it will be especially natural for you to resent disabilities that you cannot see. Physical wounds can be seen and easily accepted, but emotional reactions are more difficult to accept as injuries.

On the other hand, will you tend to be overly sympathetic? Excessive sympathy for an incapacitated person can be as harmful as negative feelings in your relationship with him. He needs strong help, but he does not need to be overwhelmed with pity.

Above all, you must guard against becoming impatient, intolerant, and resentful, or overly solicitous. Remember that such emotion in you will rarely help the victim and can never increase your ability to make clear decisions. If he can see in you calmness, confidence, and competence, he will be reassured and will feel greater security in the world around him.

The following principles should make your first-aid job easier:

- Understand that people are all different. People are the products of an enormous variety of factors. We are all different, and we don't all react the same way to the same situation. You may be impressed with how well you made it through a disaster in comparison with someone else; but there is no guarantee that the situation will not be reversed next time. The victim does not want to be upset and worried any more than you would; he would "snap out of it" if he could. Your job, therefore, is to help him in this tough situation, not to be his critic—you'd appreciate the same kind of consideration if you were in his place.

- Realize that emotional injuries are just as real as physical injuries. Such expressions as, "It's all in your head," "Snap out of it," "Buck up," and "Get a hold of yourself," are often used by people who believe they are being helpful. Actually, these goading terms are often expressions of hostility because they show a lack of understanding. They only emphasize weakness and inadequacy and are of no use in psychological first aid.

- Realize that every physically injured person has some emotional reaction to the fact that he is injured. A slight injury such as a cut finger gives most people a start. But damage to a highly valued part of the body, such as the eyes, is likely to be severely upsetting. An injured person always feels less secure, more anxious, and more afraid, not only because of what has happened to him but also because of more dire things he imagines may still happen as a result of his injury. This fear and insecurity may cause him to be irritable, stubborn, or unreasonable; he may seem uncooperative, unnecessarily difficult, or even emotionally irrational. As you help him, always keep in mind that such behavior has little or nothing to do with you personally. He needs your patience, reassurance, encouragement, and support. Even though he seems disagreeable and ungrateful at first, get across the idea that you want to help him.

- Realize that there is more strength in most disturbed people than appears at first glance. No injured or sick person puts his best foot forward. The strong points of his personality are likely to be hidden beneath his fear, anguish, and pain. It is easy to see only his failures, even though he may have worked efficiently alongside of you only a short time ago. With your aid, his "real self" will soon resurface.

Keeping these principles in mind, consider the following first-aid measures as you seek the right combination of tactics to bring about the victim's recovery:

- Getting through to the Victim. Persistent efforts to make the victim realize that you want to understand him will be reassuring. Familiar things such as the use of his name, or the sight of familiar people and activities, will add to his ability to overcome his fear and other emotional problems. By your words, attitude, and behavior, let him know of your willingness and ability to understand his feelings. Show patience and a real desire to help. He will not respond if you are excited, angry, or abrupt.

- Venting Emotions. In the terror of injury or catastrophe, many casualties give up. By being calm, patient, and willing to listen to a victim, you can get across the idea that you believe in him, that you respect him as a human being, and that you think he is worthwhile. Then perhaps he will begin to talk. There is no better medicine for fear and feelings of isolation than a chance to talk with a friendlly person. Encourage talk and be a good listener. A person will frequently solve his own problems when he is encouraged to put them into his own words and to examine how he really feels about them.

- Activity. After you help a victim get over his initial fear, regain some self-confidence, and realize that his job is to continue to function as best he can, you should then help him find something to do. Get him to help load trucks, clean up debris, or help others. Avoid having him just sit around. Your instructions to him should be clear and simple. They should be repeated, and they should be reasonable and obviously possible. A person who has panicked is likely to argue. Respect his feeling, but point out more immediate, obtainable, and demanding needs. Do not argue. If you cannot get him interested in doing something profitable, it may be necessary to enlist aid in controlling his overactivity before it spreads to the group and results in more panic.

- Rest. There are times when physical exhaustion is a principal cause of emotional reactions. For the weary disaster victim, adequate rest, warm food, and a change of clothing with an opportunity to bathe may provide spectacular results.

- Benefits of the Group Spirit. You have probably noticed that a person works better, faces danger better, and handles serious problems better in a group. Each individual in a group supports the others and seems to be strengthened in turn by the group. This group spirit is so powerful that it is one of the most effective tools you have in psychological first aid. Make sure victims do not become isolated from others and thus reinforce their emotional problems.

Finally, once you have helped the victim regain his confidence and feel more secure in the world about him, assure him that you expect him to recover fully, that there is much he can do, and that there is a pressing need for his help. Just as with the physically injured casualty, medical personnel will take over the care of the psychological casualty as soon as possible. The first aid he has received from you will be of great value to his complete recovery.

APPENDIXES

Appendix 1: Basic Home Survival Supplies

Water
Water-purification materials

Food
Multiple vitamin pills
Grinder (hand powered) for preparing flour from stored wheat

Utensils
Paper plates
Cups
Knives
Forks
Spoons
Pans
Can and bottle openers
Pocket knife
Butcher knife

Sanitation and Health
Garbage can with lid
Small can with tight lid
Plastic bags
Newspapers
Disinfectant or bleach
Soap—hand and laundry
Deodorizers
Toilet tissue
Wash pan
Towels
Emergency toilet
Combs and hairbrush
Toothbrushes and toothpaste
Washboard

Beds
Cots
Sleeping bags
Blankets

Supplies and Equipment
Disaster Survival Handbook
First-aid book
Paper and pencil
Bible and other reading material
Sewing kit

First-aid kit
Medicines
Camp stove
Fuel for stove
Firewood and / or coal
Clock (windup type)
Calendar
Water-purification tablets
Magnifying glass
Flares
Whetstone
Razor blades
Plastic electrician tape
Fishing kit (line, leader, hooks, flies, sinkers, and lures)
Aluminum foil
Steel wool (grade 00) for tinder
Plastic sheet (9' × 12')
Maps
Whistle
Surgical tubing (18'') for flippers
Matches
String and rope
Broom and dust pan
Candles
Lanterns
Crowbar
Saws (including survival wire saw)
Axe
Shovel
Wrench and pliers
Nails and screws
Hammer
Screwdriver
Hose
Radio (battery type)
Flashlight and batteries
Fire extinguisher
Games

Clothing
Store clothing appropriate for the situation and the seasons to last one year.

Appendix 2: Relief from Boredom

Human activity during and after a disaster occurrence is most strenuous. However, after a disaster, victims may have long periods in which there is little to do. Boredom sets in but can be relieved by books and games. *Readers' Digest Condensed Books,* back issues of *Readers' Digest* magazine, and paperback books are highly recommended.

The following is a list of suggested games with information about each game.

Game	Age of Players	No. of Players	Description
Checkers	6 and up	2	The classic strategy board game of capture
Chess	6 and up	2	The classic strategy board game of attack and containment.
Parcheesi	6 and up	2–4	The royal game of India moves four pawns from starting point to home.
Sorry	6 and up	2–4	The luck of the draw helps determine the winner.
UNO	7 and up	2–10	Family card game.
Clue	8 and up	3–6	A detective game that calls for common sense and powers of deduction as well as luck.
Monopoly	8 and up	2–8	Players buy, sell, build and trade properties to accumulate greater wealth and power than their opponents.
Scrabble	8 and up	2–4	The original crossword board game that requires strategy and luck. One edition, a sentence crossword, is designed for children 6–12 years old.
Risk	10 and up	2–6	World conquest is the goal as players try to move armies across countries.

Adapted from *Changing Times* magazine.

Appendix 3: Storage Chart

Food	Recommended Storage (70°F)	Handling Hints
Baking powder	18 months or expiration date on can	Keep dry and covered.

Baking soda	2 years	Keep dry and covered.
Bouillon cubes or granules	2 years	Keep dry and covered.
Cereals		
ready-to-eat (unopened)	6–12 months	
ready-to-eat (opened)	2–3 months	Refold package liner tightly after opening.
cooked	6 months	
Chocolate		
premelted	12 months	Keep cool.
semi-sweet	18 months	Keep cool.
unsweetened	18 months	Keep cool.
Chocolate syrup		
(unopened)	2 years	
(opened)	6 months	Cover tightly. Refrigerate after opening.
Cocoa mixes	8 months	Cover tightly.
Coffee		
cans (unopened)	2 years	
cans (opened)	2 weeks	
Instant (unopened)	1–2 years	
Instant (opened)	2 months	Refrigerate after opening; keep tightly closed. Use dry measuring spoon.
Coffee lighteners		
(dry) (unopened)	9 months	
(opened)	6 months	Keep tightly closed.
Cornmeal	12 months	Keep tightly closed.
Cornstarch	18 months	Keep tightly closed.
Flour, white	6–8 months	Keep in airtight container.
whole wheat	6–8 months	Keep refrigerated. Store in airtight containers.
Gelatin, all types	18 months	Keep in original container.
Grits	12 months	Store in airtight container.
Honey	12 months	Cover tightly. If crystallizes, warm jar in pan of hot water.
Jellies, jams	12 months	Cover tightly. Storage life lengthened if refrigerated after opening.

Molasses		
(unopened)	12 months	
(opened)	6 months	Keep tightly closed. Refrigerate to extend storage life.
Marshmallow		
cream (unopened)	3–4 months	Cover tightly. Refrigerate after opening to extend storage life. Serve at room temperature.
Marshmallows	2–3 months	Keep in airtight container.
Mayonnaise		
(unopened)	2–3 months	Refrigerate after opening.
Milk		
condensed or evaporated		
(unopened)	12 months	Invert cans every 2 months.
nonfat dry		
(unopened)	6 months	
(opened)	3 months	Put in airtight container.
Pasta (spaghetti, macaroni, etc.)	2 years	Once opened, store in airtight container.
Pectin, liquid		
(opened)	1 month	Recap and refrigerate.
Rice, white	2 years	Keep tightly closed.
flavored or herb	6 months	
Salad dressings		
bottled		
(unopened)	10–12 months	
bottled (opened)	3 months	Refrigerate after opening.
made from mix	2 weeks	Refrigerate prepared dressing.
Salad oils		
(unopened)	6 months	
(opened)	1–3 months	Refrigerate after opening.
Shortenings, solid	8 months	Refrigeration not needed.
Sugar		
brown	4 months	Put in airtight container.
confectioners	18 months	Put in airtight container.
granulated	2 years	Cover tightly.
artificial sweeteners	2 years	Cover tightly.

Syrups	12 months	Keep tightly closed. Refrigerate to extend storage life.
Tea		
bags	18 months	Put in airtight container.
instant	3 years	Cover tightly.
loose	2 years	Put in airtight container.
Vinegar (unopened)	2 years	
(opened)	12 months	Keep tightly closed. Slightly cloudy appearance doesn't affect quality. Distilled vinegar keeps longer than cider vinegar.

Mixes and Packaged Foods

Biscuit, brownie, muffin mix	9 months	Keep cool and dry.
Cakes, purchased	1–2 days	If butter-cream, whipped cream or custard frostings, fillings, refrigerate.
Cake mixes	9 months	Keep cool and dry.
angel food	12 months	
Casseroles, complete or add own meat	9–12 months	Keep cool and dry.
Cookies, homemade	2–3 weeks	Put in airtight container.
packaged	2 months	Keep box tightly closed.
Crackers	8 months	Keep box tightly closed.
Frosting, canned	3 months	Store leftovers in refrigerator.
mix	8 months	
Hot-roll mix	18 months	If opened, put in airtight container.
Pancake mix	6–9 months	Put in airtight container.
Piecrust mix	8 months	Keep cool and dry.
Pies and pastries	2–3 days	Refrigerate whipped cream, custard and chiffon fillings.
Potatoes, instant	6–12 months	Keep in airtight package.
Pudding mixes	12 months	Keep cool and dry.
Rice, mixes	6 months	Keep cool and dry.
Sauce and gravy mixes	6–12 months	Keep cool and dry.

Soup mixes	12 months	Keep cool and dry.
Toaster pastries	2–3 months	Keep in airtight packet.

Canned and Dried Foods

Canned foods, all (unopened)	12 months	Keep cool.
Canned fruit juices	9 months	Keep cool.
Canned foods (opened)		ALL OPENED CANNED FOODS—
baby foods	2–3 days	Refrigerate and
fish and seafood	2 days	cover tightly. To
fruit	1 week	avoid metallic taste,
meats	2 days	transfer foods in
pickles, olives	1–2 months	cans to glass or
poultry	2 days	plastic storage
sauce, tomato	5 days	containers, if kept
vegetables	3 days	more than 1 day.
Fruits, dried	6 months	Keep cool, in
Vegetables, dried	1 year	airtight containers, if possible refrigerate.

Spices, Herbs, Condiments, and Extracts

Catsup, chili sauce (unopened)	12 months	Refrigerate for longer storage.
(opened)	1 month	
Mustard, prepared		
yellow (unopened)	2 years	
(opened)	6–8 months	May be refrigerated. Stir before using.
Spices & herbs		
whole spices	1–2 years	Store in airtight
ground spices	6 months	containers in dry
herbs	6 months	places away from
herb/spice		sunlight and heat.
blends	6 months	At times listed, check aroma; if faded, replace. Whole cloves, nutmeg and cinnamon sticks maintain quality beyond 2-year period.
Vanilla (unopened)	2 years	
(opened)	12 months	Keep tightly closed. Volatile oils escape.
Other extracts		
(opened)	12 months	Keep tightly closed. Volatile oils escape.
Veget., dehyd. flakes	6 months	

Others

Cheese, Parmesan- grated (unopened) (opened)	10 months 2 months	Refrigerate after opening. Keep tightly closed.
Coconut, shredded-canned or packaged (unopened) (opened)	12 months 6 months	Refrigerate after opening.
Meat substitutes- textured protein products (e.g., imitation bacon bits)	4 months	Keep tightly closed. For longer storage, refrigerate.
Metered-caloric products, instant breakfast	6 months	Keep in can, closed jars or original packets.
Nuts in-shell (unopened)	4 months	Refrigerate after opening. Freeze for longer storage. Unsalted and blanched nuts keep longer than salted.
nutmeats packaged (unopened) vacuum can other packaging	1 year 3 months	
nutmeats (opened)	2 weeks	
Peanut butter (unopened) (opened)	6–9 months 2–3 months	Refrigeration not needed. Keeps longer if refrigerated. Use at room temperature.
Peas, beans-dried	12 months	Store in airtight container in cool place.
Popcorn	2 years	Store in airtight container.
Vegetables fresh onions	2 weeks	Keep dry and away from sun.
potatoes, white	2–4 weeks	For longer storage, keep about 50°. Don't refrigerate sweet potatoes.
sweet	1–2 weeks	
Whipped topping (dry)	12 months	Keep cool and dry.
Yeast, dry	Expiration date on package	Freeze for longer storage.

Courtesy KSL Radio (Salt Lake City) and Utah State University Extension Services. By permission.

INDEX